HANNIBAL

◆ ◆ ◆

❖ ANCIENT WORLD LEADERS ❖

ALEXANDER THE GREAT

ATTILA THE HUN

CHARLEMAGNE

CLEOPATRA

CYRUS THE GREAT

DARIUS THE GREAT

GENGHIS KHAN

HAMMURABI

HANNIBAL

JULIUS CAESAR

KING DAVID

NEFERTITI

QUEEN OF SHEBA

RAMSES THE GREAT

SALADIN

XERXES

HANNIBAL

CLIFFORD W. MILLS

CHELSEA HOUSE
PUBLISHERS
An imprint of Infobase Publishing

Frontis: Portrait of Carthaginian general Hannibal.

Hannibal
Copyright © 2008 by Infobase Publishing

Chelsea House
An imprint of Infobase Publishing
132 West 31st Street
New York, NY 10001

Library of Congress Cataloging-in-Publication Data

Mills, Cliff, 1947–
  Hannibal / Cliff Mills.
    p. cm. — (Ancient world leaders)
  Includes bibliographical references and index.
  ISBN 978-0-7910-9580-5 (hardcover)
  1. Hannibal, 247–182 B.C.—Juvenile literature. 2. Generals—Tunisia—Carthage (Extinct city)—Biography—Juvenile literature. 3. Punic War, 2nd, 218–201 B.C.—Juvenile literature. 4. Carthage (Extinct city)—History—Juvenile literature. 5. Rome—History—Republic, 265–30 B.C.—Juvenile literature. I. Title. II. Series.

  DG249.M55 2008
  937'.04092—dc22   2007050493
  [B]

Text design by Lina Farinella
Cover design by Jooyoung An
Composition by North Market Street Graphics
Cover printed by Bang Printing, Brainerd, MN
Book printed and bound by Bang Printing, Brainerd, MN
Date printed: October 2010
Printed in the United States of America

10 9 8 7 6 5 4 3 2

This book is printed on acid-free paper.

❖ CONTENTS ❖

Foreword: On Leadership   6
Arthur M. Schlesinger, Jr.

1   Preparing for a Legendary Journey   13

2   Becoming Mortal Combatants   25

3   Marching to the Alps   41

4   Slashing into Italy   54

5   Shock and Awe in Italy   65

6   A War Without Victory   75

7   War of the Worlds   93

8   Fighting to the End   102

    Chronology   111
    Bibliography   113
    Further Reading   114
    Photo Credits   115
    Index   116
    About the Authors   120

Arthur M. Schlesinger, Jr.
On Leadership

L eadership, it may be said, is really what makes the world go round. Love no doubt smoothes the passage; but love is a private transaction between consenting adults. Leadership is a public transaction with history. The idea of leadership affirms the capacity of individuals to move, inspire, and mobilize masses of people so that they act together in pursuit of an end. Sometimes leadership serves good purposes, sometimes bad; but whether the end is benign or evil, great leaders are those men and women who leave their personal stamp on history.

Now, the very concept of leadership implies the proposition that individuals can make a difference. This proposition has never been universally accepted. From classical times to the present day, eminent thinkers have regarded individuals as no more than the agents and pawns of larger forces, whether the gods and goddesses of the ancient world or, in the modern era, race, class, nation, the dialectic, the will of the people, the spirit of the times, history itself. Against such forces, the individual dwindles into insignificance.

So contends the thesis of historical determinism. Tolstoy's great novel *War and Peace* offers a famous statement of the case. Why, Tolstoy asked, did millions of men in the Napoleonic Wars, denying their human feelings and their common sense, move back and forth across Europe slaughtering their fellows? "The war," Tolstoy answered, "was bound to happen simply because it was bound to happen." All prior history determined it. As for leaders, they, Tolstoy said, "are but the labels that serve to give a name to an end and, like labels, they have the least possible connection with the event." The greater the leader, "the more conspicuous the inevitability and the predestination of every act he commits." The leader, said Tolstoy, is "the slave of history."

Determinism takes many forms. Marxism is the determinism of class. Nazism the determinism of race. But the idea of men and women as the slaves of history runs athwart the deepest human instincts. Rigid determinism abolishes the idea of human freedom—the assumption of free choice that underlies every move we make, every word we speak, every thought we think. It abolishes the idea of human responsibility, since it is manifestly unfair to reward or punish people for actions that are by definition beyond their control. No one can live consistently by any deterministic creed. The Marxist states prove this themselves by their extreme susceptibility to the cult of leadership.

More than that, history refutes the idea that individuals make no difference. In December 1931 a British politician crossing Fifth Avenue in New York City between 76th and 77th Streets around 10:30 p.m. looked in the wrong direction and was knocked down by an automobile— a moment, he later recalled, of a man aghast, a world aglare: "I do not understand why I was not broken like an eggshell or squashed like a gooseberry." Fourteen months later an American politician, sitting in an open car in Miami, Florida, was fired on by an assassin; the man beside him was hit. Those who believe that individuals make no difference to history might well ponder whether the next two decades would have been the same had Mario Constasino's car killed Winston Churchill in 1931 and Giuseppe Zangara's bullet killed Franklin Roosevelt in 1933. Suppose, in addition, that Lenin had died of typhus in Siberia in 1895 and that Hitler had been killed on the western front in 1916. What would the 20th century have looked like now?

For better or for worse, individuals do make a difference. "The notion that a people can run itself and its affairs anonymously," wrote the philosopher William James, "is now well known to be the silliest of absurdities. Mankind does nothing save through initiatives on the part of inventors, great or small, and imitation by the rest of us—these are the sole factors in human progress. Individuals of genius show the way, and set the patterns, which common people then adopt and follow."

Leadership, James suggests, means leadership in thought as well as in action. In the long run, leaders in thought may well make the greater difference to the world. "The ideas of economists and political philosophers, both when they are right and when they are wrong," wrote John Maynard Keynes, "are more powerful than is commonly understood. Indeed the world is ruled by little else. Practical men, who believe themselves to be quite exempt from any intellectual influences, are usually the slaves of some defunct economist. . . . The power of vested interests is vastly exaggerated compared with the gradual encroachment of ideas."

But, as Woodrow Wilson once said, "Those only are leaders of men, in the general eye, who lead in action. . . . It is at their hands that new thought gets its translation into the crude language of deeds." Leaders in thought often invent in solitude and obscurity, leaving to later generations the tasks of imitation. Leaders in action—the leaders portrayed in this series—have to be effective in their own time.

And they cannot be effective by themselves. They must act in response to the rhythms of their age. Their genius must be adapted, in a phrase from William James, "to the receptivities of the moment." Leaders are useless without followers. "There goes the mob," said the French politician, hearing a clamor in the streets. "I am their leader. I must follow them." Great leaders turn the inchoate emotions of the mob to purposes of their own. They seize on the opportunities of their time, the hopes, fears, frustrations, crises, potentialities. They succeed when events have prepared the way for them, when the community is awaiting to be aroused, when they can provide the clarifying and organizing ideas. Leadership completes the circuit between the individual and the mass and thereby alters history.

It may alter history for better or for worse. Leaders have been responsible for the most extravagant follies and most monstrous crimes that have beset suffering humanity. They have also been vital in such gains as humanity has made in individual freedom, religious and racial tolerance, social justice, and respect for human rights.

There is no sure way to tell in advance who is going to lead for good and who for evil. But a glance at the gallery of men and women in ANCIENT WORLD LEADERS suggests some useful tests.

One test is this: Do leaders lead by force or by persuasion? By command or by consent? Through most of history leadership was exercised by the divine right of authority. The duty of followers was to defer and to obey. "Theirs not to reason why/ Theirs but to do and die." On occasion, as with the so-called enlightened despots of the 18th century in Europe, absolutist leadership was animated by humane purposes. More often, absolutism nourished the passion for domination, land, gold, and conquest and resulted in tyranny.

The great revolution of modern times has been the revolution of equality. "Perhaps no form of government," wrote the British historian James Bryce in his study of the United States, *The American Commonwealth*, "needs great leaders so much as democracy." The idea that all people should be equal in their legal condition has undermined the old structure of authority, hierarchy, and deference. The revolution of equality has had two contrary effects on the nature of leadership. For equality, as Alexis de Tocqueville pointed out in his great study *Democracy in America*, might mean equality in servitude as well as equality in freedom.

"I know of only two methods of establishing equality in the political world," Tocqueville wrote. "Rights must be given to every citizen, or none at all to anyone . . . save one, who is the master of all." There was no middle ground "between the sovereignty of all and the absolute power of one man." In his astonishing prediction of 20th-century totalitarian dictatorship, Tocqueville explained how the revolution of equality could lead to the *Führerprinzip* and more terrible absolutism than the world had ever known.

But when rights are given to every citizen and the sovereignty of all is established, the problem of leadership takes a new form, becomes more exacting than ever before. It is easy to issue commands and enforce them by the rope and the stake, the concentration camp and the *gulag*. It is much harder to use argument and achievement to overcome opposition and win consent. The Founding Fathers of the United States understood the difficulty. They believed that history had given them the opportunity to decide, as Alexander Hamilton wrote in the first Federalist Paper, whether men are indeed capable of basing government on "reflection and choice, or whether they are forever destined to depend . . . on accident and force."

Government by reflection and choice called for a new style of leadership and a new quality of followership. It required leaders to be responsive to popular concerns, and it required followers to be active and informed participants in the process. Democracy does not eliminate emotion from politics; sometimes it fosters demagoguery; but it is confident that, as the greatest of democratic leaders put it, you cannot fool all of the people all of the time. It measures leadership by results and retires those who overreach or falter or fail.

It is true that in the long run despots are measured by results too. But they can postpone the day of judgment, sometimes indefinitely, and in the meantime they can do infinite harm. It is also true that democracy is no guarantee of virtue and intelligence in government, for the voice of the people is not necessarily the voice of God. But democracy, by assuring the right of opposition, offers built-in resistance to the evils inherent in absolutism. As the theologian Reinhold Niebuhr summed it up, "Man's capacity for justice makes democracy possible, but man's inclination to justice makes democracy necessary."

A second test for leadership is the end for which power is sought. When leaders have as their goal the supremacy of a master race or the promotion of totalitarian revolution or the acquisition and exploitation of colonies or the protection of greed and privilege or the preservation of personal power, it is likely that their leadership will do little to advance the cause of humanity. When their goal is the abolition of slavery, the liberation of women, the enlargement of opportunity for the poor and powerless, the extension of equal rights to racial minorities, the defense of the freedoms of expression and opposition, it is likely that their leadership will increase the sum of human liberty and welfare.

Leaders have done great harm to the world. They have also conferred great benefits. You will find both sorts in this series. Even "good" leaders must be regarded with a certain wariness. Leaders are not demigods; they put on their trousers one leg after another just like ordinary mortals. No leader is infallible, and every leader needs to be reminded of this at regular intervals. Irreverence irritates leaders but is their salvation. Unquestioning submission corrupts leaders and demeans followers. Making a cult of a leader is always a mistake. Fortunately, hero worship generates its own antidote. "Every hero," said Emerson, "becomes a bore at last."

The single benefit the great leaders confer is to embolden the rest of us to live according to our own best selves, to be active, insistent, and resolute in affirming our own sense of things. For great leaders attest to the reality of human freedom against the supposed inevitabilities of history. And they attest to the wisdom and power that may lie within the most unlikely of us, which is why Abraham Lincoln remains the supreme example of great leadership. A great leader, said Emerson, exhibits new possibilities to all humanity. "We feed on genius. . . . Great men exist that there may be greater men."

Great leaders, in short, justify themselves by emancipating and empowering their followers. So humanity struggles to master its destiny, remembering with Alexis de Tocqueville: "It is true that around every man a fatal circle is traced beyond which he cannot pass; but within the wide verge of that circle he is powerful and free; as it is with man, so with communities." ◆

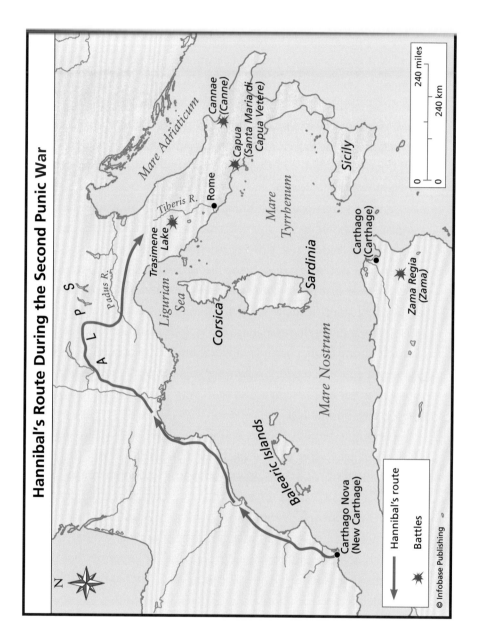

Hannibal's Route During the Second Punic War

© Infobase Publishing

1

Preparing for a Legendary Journey

THE EARLY SPRING SUN WARMED THE ROCKY CLIFFS ABOVE THE DEEP BLUE waters of the western Mediterranean Sea. High on those cliffs overlooking the ancient city of New Carthage were several palaces, also warmed by the rising sun. The city was perched on top of the eastern shores of the Iberian Peninsula, near where Spain's city of Cartagena is today. The palaces and the city terraces gleamed in the morning light, and children raced the streets knowing that something important was happening. The year was 218 B.C.

A strong and dark young man with piercing black eyes looked down from one of the palaces. He glanced out to the shimmering waves far below, and then to the silver olive groves and brown fields stretching away from the sea. The man watched several workers plowing the fields, getting the ground ready for the upcoming spring planting. His name was Hannibal Barca. He was just 28 years old, but with the deaths of his father, Hamilcar, and his brother-in-law Hasdrupal, he had become the military leader of one of the greatest civilizations in ancient history— the Carthaginians. This North African culture had expanded to Iberia (today's Spain and Portugal) and had founded the city of New Carthage to extend its influence beyond Africa.

On this spring day, as he was surveying all he knew in the city, Hannibal was making preparations before setting out on one of the greatest and most dangerous adventures in human history. He had an important speech to give, and he must have been thinking about just what he needed to say and how he needed to say it. He had to prepare an army for war, and he had to vow to protect his family, his fellow citizens, and his civilization.

PLANNING FOR WAR

That day in New Carthage, Hannibal knew that a rising power in the ancient world, the city of Rome and its allies, had declared war on Carthage and its territories. A clash of civilizations had been inevitable as the rising power in Rome challenged the established power of Carthage for economic and military supremacy of the Mediterranean world and beyond. Hannibal, as a leader of Carthage and New Carthage, did not wait for diplomats to interpret terms of existing treaties or to try to negotiate terms of peace. He had grown up with war, and he had vowed to his father that he would fight the Romans for the rest of his life. His destiny was war. He was born in a time when war was not something to be avoided, but rather a way for individuals and societies to prove their strength and honor.

No one knows when Hannibal formed a plan for the most daring military strike in world history. His father, a great general, had taught him to think in the boldest terms. Hannibal

Carthage, now in ruins, was the base of one of the most powerful ancient civilizations, with territories in Africa, Spain, and Portugal. When Carthage began to expand, it brought the Carthaginians in direct conflict with the other great civilization of the time: Rome.

himself would become known as the father of military strategy. His plan was both very simple and very complicated. He would march a large army over two mountain ranges and attack Rome by land, something no one thought possible. The ancient world knew that Carthage had a great navy and had fought all of its great battles using that navy. The two mountain ranges, the Pyrenees bordering Iberia and France, and the Alps, bordering France and Italy, were vast and imposing walls—especially the Alps. Attacking Rome from the northwest and through the mountains, rather than from the south by sea, was a plan so far-fetched that it defied imagination.

Fearing that Rome would eventually attack Carthage in North Africa and New Carthage in Iberia, Hannibal must have felt that he would rather bring war to the Romans than have them bring it to him and his people. He knew he would

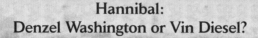

Hannibal: Denzel Washington or Vin Diesel?

The success of the movie *Gladiator* in 2000 led movie companies to plan many more "sword-and-sandal" movies. The story of Hannibal Barca is made for Hollywood. The first decision a casting director has to make is whether to cast someone like Denzel Washington, who is black, or someone like Vin Diesel, who is not, to play the lead role. Some historians point out that Hannibal has been a black hero for the ages, coming from Africa. Others say ancient North Africans would have been Semitic whites from Phoenicia. Still others say that intermarriage would have produced a range of skin colors and facial features.

always be outnumbered by the growing and sprawling Roman civilization and armies. He had to surprise them. He knew they expected him to attack by sea, if he did attack. The Romans would prepare for his navy. In fact, they had already prepared by building an enormous navy of their own.

Hannibal knew that Italy was dominated by Rome but that the country still had many city-states and tribes only loosely tied to Rome. He reasoned that, if he could challenge Roman power and authority, some of these states and tribes would be won over to his cause. After all, some of them must have resented the new grab for domination by Rome and its brutally efficient legions. Hannibal had heard from his scouts that the fierce warriors between the two mountain ranges, the Gauls, might be willing to join his army. Some already had. He knew that some of their leaders would follow him.

Judging from ancient coins, it appears that Hannibal was more Vin Diesel than Denzel Washington. There is no question, however, that ancient North Africa was racially diverse, and Hannibal probably had some black ancestors. Casting directors know that audiences feel strongly about how people are portrayed. They would probably want a racially ambiguous star to play Hannibal, which argues for Vin Diesel, or even the Rock (ex-professional wrestler Dwayne Johnson, who is Samoan and black). Both would have the physical power to represent Hannibal well.

A truism about Hollywood is that, after everything is said and done, more is said than done. Meanwhile, the conquerors of the ancient world remain hard to cast. The director of the 1956 movie *The Conqueror* cast John Wayne in the role of Genghis Kahn, setting a very low standard of realistic racial portrayals.

Hannibal also knew that, for his grand plan to work, he had to cross the higher mountain range, the Alps, before winter set in. He needed guides to get him through the mountains. The Gauls could help in many ways. He now needed to complete his recruiting of an army. He sent his emissaries for war everywhere.

BUILDING A GREAT ARMY FROM MANY SMALL ONES

One day in the early spring of 218 B.C., Hannibal, his wife, Imilce, and his young son watched the last of the soldiers come to New Carthage from all over the Iberian Peninsula and northern Africa. Hannibal knew some of the soldiers; they had fought with him and his father in a previous war with the Romans. They formed a core of the veteran army. Some were from Carthage itself, including all of the officers. But he did not know most of the new army—a group of "silver spears," or mercenaries who had come to New Carthage from all directions to join up for plunder and glory. These professional soldiers had no loyalty to a country. The only thing that bound them to an army was loyalty to their commander, and his promise to deliver the rewards of victory. The people of Carthage did not want many of their own sons to die for their country. They could hire others to fight.

Some of the mercenaries were tribesmen from Iberia, many wearing light armor and carrying a short Spanish sword, a shield, and a spear. They had been enemies of Hamilcar but now saw the chance for victory and its many gifts, large and small. Some were Gauls from southern France. Some were from Greece and carried heavy armor and weapons. A few soldiers in the growing army came from the Balearic Islands off the eastern coast of Spain. They were called "slingers" because they used both long and short slings to throw pebbles and rocks at their enemies. They could sling both overhanded and underhanded (like a softball pitcher), and they had grown up perfecting their skills. Many historians estimate that the rocks thrown from a sling traveled faster than arrows and could crush skulls. The biblical story of David and Goliath captures their power. The Balearic Islands slingers were the best in the ancient world at their deadly craft, and they demanded payment not in gold but in captive women.

Perhaps the most important component of the army assembling in New Carthage in the spring of 218 B.C. to fight the Romans was African horsemen called Numidians. The word *nomad* derives from their name; Berber tribesmen are their direct descendants. Numidia stretched for some 700 miles along the western African coast, near where Algeria is today. The hilly countryside made the horsemen expert riders in difficult terrain, and their small horses were fast, light, and maneuverable. The Numidians could ride with or without a bridle and had complete control over their horses with just leg pressure. When the horsemen came at opposing armies with blinding speed and piercing javelins, they were a devastating force. They could retreat from harm's way just as quickly as they assaulted. They were experts in camouflage as well, making them even more dangerous.

The most well-known component of Hannibal's new army was a kind of ancient tank, the elephant. His army probably used African elephants that stood about eight feet high at the shoulder. However, the elephant Hannibal rode over the Alps was named Surus, or "the Syrian," and was probably a larger Indian elephant imported from Syria through Egypt. The elephants needed special handlers, but historians think some of the Numidians also knew how to control the animals. Hannibal's soldiers used the "armored" elephants (the animals were protected with special shields and often carried small towers so their riders could see and shoot better) just as a modern army would use a tank—as protection when needed, and as an assault weapon when possible. Unlike tanks, however, elephants could panic and trample their own army.

Hannibal's use of elephants to cross the Pyrenees and the Alps set a new precedent for bold thinking in warfare. Elephants used in battle provided transportation for men and supplies, but were also destructive against enemy forces.

The smaller bands of men growing into a large army needed a strong leader. They were not natural followers. Those who knew Hannibal realized he was a commanding presence, fearless, and tireless. The ancient historian Livy gives a portrait of the young Hannibal:

He was perfectly cool. . . . No toil could weary his body or conquer his spirit. Heat and cold he bore with equal patience. . . . Many saw him, wrapped in military cloak, lying on the ground amidst the sentries and pickets. . . . Of all the cavalry and infantry, he was by far the first soldier, earliest to join the battle and last to leave it.

His new soldiers would get to know how extraordinary their leader actually was.

Warfare had changed since prehistoric tribes threw rocks at one another. Soldiers in 218 B.C. did not have many more weapons than soldiers in 1000 B.C., but they did have better organization. Carthage was a civilization like ancient Mesopotamia—it grew enough crops that a surplus was created. Ruling elites emerged, and these elites were often led by military families. The Barca family was a commanding family. Hannibal was the family member most destined for greatness.

A SPEECH LIKE THUNDER

With a blast of trumpets and the sun reflecting off his armor, Hannibal walked out in front of the tens of thousands of soldiers. He climbed up to a massive podium and raised his hand for silence. Interpreters waited to translate each word into Iberian, Greek, and Numidian. Hannibal began by proclaiming that Carthage and Rome were at war. He told the soldiers they would march northward across the Pyrenees and the Alps and take the battle to the gates of Rome. Hannibal described the great wealth of the lands they would cross, wealth that would be theirs for the taking. The Italian fields were filled with corn, and their vineyards filled with grapes for wine. The Italian women were beautiful. It was all to be theirs. He also described the help they would receive from the Gauls and others.

The men roared their approval. They, of course, did not realize the difficulties they would face. Hannibal went on to say that their campaign would not be easy, but that they would walk in triumph when they returned home. Hannibal praised their fighting spirit and the need to conquer Rome. As his words rippled back through the crowds, both the soldiers and citizens of New Carthage roared even louder. Tens of thousands of shouts, pounding feet, and clanging weapons drowned out any other sound. The clamor rolled down to the sea. Nearby fishermen must have thought they were hearing thunder from a sky without clouds.

Hannibal then gave the men a date to reassemble in New Carthage and told them to go home to their families until then. He walked off the podium and into the arms of his wife and son. As the soldiers left New Carthage for their homes, they could

Revealing Sources

There are various sources for material about the story of Hannibal and his exploits. The most comprehensive is from a Greek historian named Polybius, who wrote a history of Rome after being arrested in 168 B.C. when Rome conquered Greece. For some reason, he had access to treaties, memoirs, speeches, and private documents from several Roman families. He was fascinated by the Punic Wars (he was born at the end of the Second Punic War and lived through the third) and interviewed many people who had been part of the events. Several Roman historians also mention the name of a young Greek who was the official historian for Hannibal. His name was Silenus, and he ventured over the Alps with the army and recorded events each day. His writings were lost or destroyed centuries ago.

A second source of material about Hannibal is coins and their inscriptions. Ancient coins provide important clues about the events of their time. Some Spanish coins have faces that experts believe are of Hannibal and his family members. The amount and quality of the silver and gold in the coins tell much about the prosperity of the times.

not have known that only one in four of them would survive the oncoming journey and war.

THE ENDLESS COLUMN

Finally, the day to reassemble in New Carthage arrived, in the late spring of 218 B.C. Historians speculate that the army formed into a column some ten men wide and seven miles long. Among the 100,000 men were 12,000 horses and 37 elephants. The nearly 90,000 foot soldiers and 12,000 cavalry got into formation. Thousands of mules and oxen that carried

A third source of information is the inscriptions taken from monuments built at the time. Most of the surviving examples are Roman. Some inscriptions are found on rock walls and milestones. Carvings on columns mark battle scenes and military campaigns.

A fourth source should be archaeological evidence, but there is precious little that relates directly to Hannibal. Many years ago, a farmer in France found elephant bones while plowing his field. A marker was raised on the spot. Unfortunately, both the bones and marker have now disappeared. There are frequent stories of strange bones found in high Alpine passes, but somehow the bones make their way into private collections before being examined by trained archaeologists.

The relatively new field of forensic archaeology may help. By using small fragments of preserved bone from ancient sites, forensic archaeologists have been trying to recreate whole skulls, including those of King Midas and Philip of Macedonia, father of Alexander the Great. The field is still controversial but fascinating nonetheless. If some of those bones found high in the Alps fall into the right hands . . .

food, supplies, battering rams, and catapults waded into the river of humanity.

Near the end of the seemingly endless and winding column was a group of some 15,000 merchants, cobblers, and blacksmiths. They would sell cooking utensils, repair shoes and boots, and fix broken weapons. Some of them would pay for or steal whatever valuables could be found on dead bodies that piled up during the battles to come. They were the human scavengers. The final group in the endless column was made up of slaves, prostitutes, and laborers. They would be used, worn out, and left to die once they became sick or tired.

Not since Alexander the Great assembled an army to march into the Persian Empire some 150 years earlier had such a concentration of fighting forces come together. By dawn's early light, Hannibal mounted Surus, held high a blazing torch, and headed the column northward toward the Pyrenees and Gaul. He could not know as he turned away from New Carthage, and his wife and son, that he would not see them again for 17 years. During that time, his leadership would change world history.

CHAPTER

2

Becoming
Mortal
Combatants

THE ANCIENT WORLD SAW MANY GREAT CIVILIZATIONS RISE AND FALL, AND
Phoenicia was one of the greatest. The Phoenicians lived mainly
on the coastal plains of what is now the country of Lebanon.
While other civilizations around them failed from disease,
volcanic eruptions, earthquakes, crop failures, and starvation,
the Phoenicians became wealthy by using the resources of the
vast Mediterranean Sea. They became great sailors, harvesting
the enormous cedar trees from their land to make the world's
finest ships. They took seashells and crushed them to make a
purple dye. They then made brilliantly colored fabrics that the
rest of the world wanted. They created the first transparent
glass, which some say was inspired by the clear waters of the
Mediterranean.

The Phoenicians were fearless explorers of the sea and coasts. From 1200 to 800 B.C., they settled many colonies around the Mediterranean—city-state ports all linked by maritime trade between Phoenicia, Mesopotamia, Egypt, and Arabia. One of these colonies was called Kardt-Hadash, meaning "new city." We now know that city as Carthage. This port was important because it was on an outcropping of North African land that narrowed the Mediterranean across from the island of Sicily. Anyone who wanted to control trade in the region wanted to control these pieces of land and sea.

THE LEGEND OF ELISSA

Historians have not been able to confirm exactly who founded Carthage. One legend tells of an intelligent and beautiful noble-woman named Elissa (also called Dido) who was living in the Phoenician city of Tyre. Her brother was the ruler and cruel tyrant of the city, and her husband a very wealthy nobleman who may have been a threat for the leadership of Tyre. Elissa's brother, according to the legend, killed her husband. Elissa escaped Tyre with all her wealth—chests full of gold and silver. She had many followers who also wanted to escape her mur-derous and tyrannical brother. They stole ships and sailed west, and Elissa and her small band of followers landed on the shores of what is now Tunisia. She was captivated by the beauty of that land. Perhaps also taken with its strategic location across from Sicily, she decided to settle there.

An African chief in the area was amazed that a woman led the band of people. He mocked her and said she could take all the land that would fit into the hide of a bull. She agreed to his terms and ordered a bull to be sacrificed. She and her followers then sliced the hide into thin strips and made a very fine thread from the strips. The thread stretched for many miles. Elissa out-lined the land she had chosen and became queen of Carthage. The chief was furious at being fooled and put a curse on the new leader.

The same legend tells of a young Trojan prince named Aeneas who fled from the Greeks and landed in Carthage. He and Elissa fell in love, and she called him her husband. They lived together in the queen's palace, but after a year, Aeneas sailed away from Carthage's harbor in the dawn's early light to meet his destiny as one of the founders of Rome. Elissa raged against her lover and then committed suicide. A medieval saying captured Elissa's fate forever: "One husband caused thy flight by dying/The other caused thy death by flying." According to the legend, among her dying breaths was a curse that destined Carthage and Rome to fight to the death. This curse would ultimately come true.

CARTHAGE RISING

Historians disagree about how much truth the legend of Elissa holds, but archaeological evidence shows that Carthage was founded around 800 B.C. (perhaps 814 B.C.), most certainly by people from Tyre. Carthage rapidly became an important trading center, or *emporia*. Valuable metals such as gold, tin, silver, iron, and copper came from all over northern Africa and Iberia and were stored in warehouses at Carthage before being loaded on to ships bound for Tyre. Ivory and hides of animals were shipped to Carthage from the coast of Africa. Elephants came from central Africa. Pottery and marble were imported from Greece. Weapons, linens, and wool were traded. Carthaginian merchants bought low and sold high. Many homes began to appear high on the hills overlooking the sea.

When the Babylonian king Nebuchadnezzar conquered Tyre in 575 B.C., many citizens fled to Carthage, helping make it the largest and wealthiest city in the ancient world by 400 B.C. Ancient historians called it "the jewel of the Mediterranean." One of the keys to its success was its sudden population growth; another was its double harbor. Natural formations and human engineers formed two harbors at Carthage. One was used for merchant ships, and the other for warships. Thus, repairing warships in dry docks did not interfere with trade. Storms and

Elissa, also known as Dido, the mythical founder and queen of Carthage, was immortalized in the famous ode *The Aeneid*, written by Roman poet Virgil. The epic poem describes the journey of Aeneas, who falls in love with Dido. After Aeneas leaves her, Dido kills herself with his sword.

pirates did little harm in either of the harbors. The city seemed blessed by nature, by its citizens' capacity for commerce and hard work (and the hard work of slaves), and by their gods.

Carthaginians built an enormous fort on one of the hills overlooking the harbors, with walls thicker than any seen in the ancient world. They built splendid temples to their gods and lavish palaces for their nobles. Like the Phoenicians before them, they built trading ports around the Mediterranean, and they became the center of the trading world. Their only competition was from the Greeks, but the western Mediterranean was of less importance to the Greeks than Persia and lands to their east. While Romans lived in small mud huts on hills overlooking the Tiber River, the Carthaginians spread into larger and larger palaces, and more and more lands.

Unlike the Phoenicians, they did not rely just on the sea. The land around Carthage had rich soil and thick forests. Plantations grew up in the countryside, and crops, cattle, horses, and sheep appeared. The rising Carthaginians used slave labor to work the land. Unlike the later Romans, the Carthaginians conquered provinces and then ruled them without mercy or a hint of freedom for the citizens. This practice would eventually help doom their society. When there are not enough free and loyal citizens to defend the homeland, to give their lives for it, a society is weakened from within. Slavery always undermined the societies that used it. Yet, for over 100 years, Carthaginians were masters of the Mediterranean.

A BOLD NEW RIVAL

In 509 B.C., something happened that changed the world forever. The small city of Rome, in the province of Latium, overthrew its tyrant king and organized into a form of government called a republic. The city was run not by a king with unlimited powers but by a group with more limited powers: a senate and two consuls, who were elected. Gradually, all social classes—including wealthy landowners, farmers, and workers—had at least some influence on what the city did to its citizens and to others. The idea was borrowed from the Greeks, but it was fitted to the new circumstances of the Italian peninsula.

The villages and cities around Rome were drawn into alliances with this new form of government. Their people would be protected from barbarians and enjoy the benefit of trading for things they wanted if they joined the Roman alliance. They would not be conquered and killed or become slaves. In fact, people would be granted a form of Roman citizenship, including most of the benefits of being Roman. As a result, the alliances widened. Eventually, neighboring cities and towns had no choice but to join; they could not survive otherwise. Therefore, through treaty or conquest, the small city of Rome widened its influence, especially toward the middle and southern parts of the Italian peninsula. It was no longer just a refuge for runaway slaves and criminals, as it had been early in its history. Over time, the number of "Romans" increased dramatically. By 300 B.C., Rome was a force to be reckoned with. Its armies were not yet professional, but each citizen had to serve at least some time as a soldier. After 100 B.C., Roman armies would become fully professional, with service requirements of 25 years. But the Roman citizen-soldiers of 300 B.C. were well trained, highly disciplined and organized, and dedicated to their city's independence.

THE FIRST WAR

Many historians think war between the two powers, Carthage and Rome, was inevitable for economic and political reasons. Each wanted to rule the Mediterranean shipping lanes and control its destiny. Others think there may be something in human nature that acts as a kind of psychological trap. If one group has something it wants to keep, it may decide by some "logic" that it needs to defend what it has by attacking others. The group is not naturally aggressive, but its logic makes it aggressive. Groups form alliances, and—when those alliances are big enough—the groups go looking for an enemy.

For whatever reasons, and no doubt there were many, the Romans decided in 264 B.C. that they would attack Carthage by attacking its people (and others) on the island of Sicily.

Victories at Sea

Historians debate the subject of the first sea battle. Most agree that the first recorded naval battle occurred about 1210 B.C. between the Hittites—led by King Suppiluliuma II—and a fleet from Cyprus. The Hittites burned all of the ships from Cyprus and won the battle. Various drawings from the ancient world show Phoenician fighting ships, each with two levels of oars and a ramming device at the front of the ship. Most scholars agree that the rowers in such boats were packed in tightly, with the noses of the rowers on one level pressed very close to the rear ends of the rowers above them. Finding good rowers became a challenge.

Naval warfare came into its own when the Greek city-states fought one another, and Athens realized it could defend itself better with a navy than an army. Yet, until the wars between Carthage and Rome, most navies were used to supply armies—not to fight large battles. Most ships in the ancient world were fit for sailing on rivers, lakes, and seas, but they were not yet ready for oceangoing voyages. Tar and pitch were not yet used on ships, so the wood became saturated and the ship became heavier and heavier with age. The only way to dry the wood and lighten the ship was to beach it, and that was when it became most vulnerable to attack; that is how Sparta defeated Athens in 405 B.C., when the Spartans surprised the beached Athenians and burned their fleet. Of course, there were no cannons or missiles to fire broadside, as would happen many centuries later, and no specialized naval tactics and coordination.

Carthage had the world's most powerful navy for many years before the First Punic War (264 B.C. to 241 B.C.). That war saw Rome rise as a naval power, and with naval power came world power. Rome later used its navy more for fighting pirates than for fighting its enemies.

As important as navies became, wars were mostly fought on land in the ancient world. An enemy was not beaten until its army was defeated on land. The Romans never relied too much on advancing their art of naval warfare, but they never needed to. Their legionnaires saw to that.

Carthage did not want war with Rome. Carthaginians were mostly businessmen, and they knew war was very expensive and bad for (most) businesses. Yet Carthage found itself in a war, and it would use its powerful navy—the world's finest—to try to overcome Rome's land forces, the famous legions. Its tactics were to retreat to coastal towns in Sicily and then fight mostly naval battles.

The deadliest ships in the world were Carthage's quinqueremes, single-deck ships with roughly 60 oars each. Each oar was pulled by five men. The ships were slow but very heavy, and they were able to ram other ships and smash them to bits. The Romans had no such weapon, but one day they found an abandoned quinquereme onshore in northern Sicily. The Romans took it apart board by board and shipped each piece back to Rome to make a model for new ship construction. Within months, Rome had many of its own quinqueremes. All the Romans needed was someone who could sail them. For that, they recruited Greeks.

For much of the war, Carthage remained superior in naval fighting because of its generations of sailing experience and knowledge of the sea. Once again, however, the Romans proved resourceful. If they couldn't win naval battles, even with their new ships, they would find a way to turn naval battles into hand-to-hand combat, at which their soldiers excelled. They invented something called a *corvus* (meaning "crow"), a wide and heavy plank of wood with a spike at one end. The corvus was dropped on to a Carthaginian ship, attaching it to the Roman ship. Soldiers could then race over the plank to slash at their Carthaginian enemies. A sea battle turned into a land battle.

The Carthaginians adapted to the new technique, helped by the fact that a corvus was so heavy that it actually capsized some of the Roman ships that carried one. This was probably the case in two separate great Mediterranean storms—in 255 B.C. and 253 B.C.—when much of the Roman fleet was destroyed in high seas.

Rome attempted to seize control of Carthage-controlled shipping routes by declaring war against Carthage and raising a navy whose size and skill would rival and overwhelm its enemy.

In one famous battle, Roman admiral Claudius Pulcher moved into position to fight a Carthaginian fleet near the port of Drepana. Claudius had to consult his high priests before going to battle, as most Roman leaders would, and the priests told him that the sacred chickens on board were not eating, so he shouldn't fight. That was a bad omen. Claudius was impatient, threw the chickens overboard, and began the fight. The corvus technique failed that day, as Carthage's ships outmaneuvered the Roman ships. Carthage won a key victory. Claudius was sent back to Rome and put on trial for his failure. He was fined heavily. If he had been Carthaginian, he would have been crucified high on a hill for all to see.

HAMILCAR BARCA

The war with Rome over Sicily came to be called the First Punic War (264 B.C.–241 B.C.). (The word *Punic* comes from the Roman name for the Carthaginians, *Punici*. The Roman name refers to the Carthaginian's origins in Phoenicia, which were named *Poenici*.) Few heroes emerged on either side as the war dragged on for more than 20 years without a clear-cut winner. Neither side could establish an advantage because neither side had a navy powerful enough to enforce blockades. As a result, armies could be resupplied and continue fighting.

There were two war heroes on the Carthaginian side, however. One was a Spartan mercenary called Xanthippus, who reorganized the Carthaginian army and navy. The other was Hamilcar Barca, who was responsible for many of the strategies and tactics that worked in fighting Rome almost to a standstill. He perfected the art of guerrilla raids along the Italian coastline, striking fear in every city near the sea. He was a strong and decisive leader of thousands of mercenaries. The name *Barca* meant "lightning" and was given to him as a tribute to the speed of his attacks. It became a kind of last name, which his sons inherited as well (although it is not a family name in the sense that the modern Western world uses). If he had received more help from his government and from private citizens in Carthage, he most certainly would have defeated the Romans in Sicily.

Carthage saw the war as unwinnable. Both armies and navies were funded by public money that was taken from ordinary citizens in taxes and fines. When the Romans ran out of public money, several rich Romans donated vast sums of money to rebuild their army and navy. No rich Carthaginians did the same, despite the vast wealth the city and its nobles possessed. Rome would prove time and again that is was more dedicated as a society to gaining and keeping world power.

Rome and Carthage eventually signed a peace treaty, with Carthage agreeing to remove its citizens and troops from Sicily. Both sides had lost in the war, but Carthage lost more. It had not wanted this war, and it was now much poorer because of the disruption of trade and the losses of ships. Much of its wealth was gone. The government in Carthage created an enormous problem for itself when it refused to pay its own mercenaries as they came home from Sicily. They had not won the war, so they would not be paid. Many mercenaries revolted and threatened the city. The conflict came to be known as the Mercenary War.

Their former leader, Hamilcar Barca, was told to put down the revolt, and he did so with troops loyal to him, helped by specially trained elephants that charged and crushed many of the rebels. Hamilcar was made commander of all the Carthaginian armies, and he became one of the most powerful men in the city. He was still stung by the war with Rome and vowed he would get revenge some day.

In 238 B.C., the government in Carthage let Hamilcar lead a large force to the Iberian Peninsula in search of gold, silver, and territory to help restore some of the wealth that Carthage lost during the First Punic War. Expanding east and north was no longer possible because of the Romans, so westward expansion was the only choice. Before leaving for Iberia, Hamilcar took part in a sacred ritual designed to bring him success: A human victim was sacrificed. Hamilcar brought his oldest son, Hannibal, to the altar and made him feel the steaming insides of the dead body. Hamilcar made his son swear that he would always be an enemy to Rome. One report states that Hannibal said, "I swear so soon as age will permit I will use fire and steel to arrest the destiny of Rome." Hannibal was only nine years old (and eloquent for someone that age). It was an oath he lived up to for the rest of his life. Hamilcar then asked his son if he wanted to sail to Spain with him. Hannibal nodded eagerly.

THE YOUNG HANNIBAL—A BORN WARRIOR

Hannibal was born in Carthage in 246 B.C., into one of the more powerful families of the ancient world. His father was a great general, and his older brother-in-law Hasdrupal was as well. The Barcas had known wealth and influence for generations. Hamilcar and his son Hannibal could have been wealthy businessmen, but both chose the life of the soldier. Hannibal's military training would have started very early, probably as soon as he could hold a small sword. He was also given the best tutoring of the time—Greek teachers who taught him many subjects, including their language. He was exposed to Greek ideas on mathematics, science, and philosophy. Some Greeks were skeptics, or people who wanted to question all received wisdom. Hannibal seemed to have learned the art of thinking clearly and always asking questions.

A legend grew up around Hannibal as a small boy. The legend tells of his hunting in the mountains around Carthage and coming upon an eagle's nest. He surprised the eagle and clutched it to his chest. The eagle clawed him, but he refused to let it go. It dragged him away from the nest to the edge of the cliff, but he still refused to let go, ignoring the pain of the talons and the beak piercing him. The eagle finally gave up the struggle, and

Hamilcar developed a deep dislike toward the Roman Empire, a hatred he passed down to his son Hannibal. This painting depicts Hamilcar asking Hannibal to swear his hatred against the Romans.

Hannibal let it go free. The young Hannibal then shouted with joy, a cry heard down the valley and into the city.

Soon, Hannibal went to Spain to be with his father and to be trained as both a soldier and a leader. He left behind the rest of his family—his mother, Didobal; his older sister, Sapanibal; his younger sister, Sophonisba; and his brothers Hanno, Mago, and Hadsrubal. Hannibal watched and then helped Hamilcar and his troops methodically conquer one tribe after another. The Celtic tribes in Iberia had intermarried with various native Iberian tribes, and their offspring were a particularly violent people known as Celtiberians. It was said that they cleaned their teeth with blood. These warriors knew no fear, but they were also undisciplined and hated to take orders. They had the finest weapons of the age, however: sharp knives and swords made with the best metal techniques in the known world. The Carthaginians used the Celtiberians as a natural resource, just as they did the gold and silver of the area. Spain had many treasures, and Carthage began to grow rich again in only a few years.

One day in 229 B.C., Hannibal was with his father in the hills of Spain when they were descended on by a group of hostile Celtiberians. Hamilcar must have recognized the danger instantly, and he sent his son down one trail while he led the enemy tribesmen down another trail. He tried to cross a river swollen from recent storms, and he was swept off his horse and drowned. We do not know whether Hannibal saw any of this, but from that day forward he became a leader, not just a soldier. He was only 17—and he did not assume formal command of Carthage's troops in Spain for several more years—but no one doubted his day was coming. He had always had his father's spirit, and now he had his father's authority as well. He had been a small spark, and he now became a raging fire.

After the death of his father, Hannibal assumed more control of his life and sought even more education. He surrounded himself with teachers who knew Latin, the language of his enemy. He learned as much as he could about Roman customs. He also threw himself into learning more about Spain and the tribes that had cost his father his life. He was going to be a leader in both thought and action, and he made learning a lifelong habit.

Soon, he was old enough to marry. He did not, however, make comfortable and easy choices. He chose not to marry a Carthaginian and instead married the daughter of a Celtic leader. Her name was Imilce, and they started a family immediately. The marriage also gave him a deeper bond to the culture he lived in, as well as many local alliances. He was growing up in every way and was now a commanding presence.

TAKING COMMAND

Hannibal was trained to be a skilled fighter both on and off a horse. He was able to discipline himself so that he could sleep for days on bare ground, eat very little, and withstand any hardship. He insisted on wearing simple armor—not the elaborate pieces he would be allowed by his heritage. He developed a charisma that was hard to define, and older soldiers said he reminded them of his father.

In 221 B.C., the Carthaginian government confirmed Hannibal as the commander of all forces after his brother-in-law Hadsrupal was killed by one of his own servants. Hannibal's first act was to subdue the very tribes in Spain that may have caused the death of his father years before. Soon, few tribes dared face him and his troops. Virtually all of Spain became part of the Carthage Empire. Wealth poured back into Carthage in North Africa, and Hannibal (now joined by his whole family) was the most prestigious Carthaginian.

The Romans took notice. They sent a delegation to New Carthage to demand that Hannibal not expand the empire any further. Hannibal met with the Roman delegation and told them that they would never dictate terms to him. The Romans warned that the Spanish city of Saguntum in the middle of the Iberian Peninsula and across the Ebro River was theirs, and any attack on it would be an attack on Rome. The Romans left, worrying that they had not been heard. They knew that this son of Hamilcar Barca was an angry young man. They may not have known about the oath he swore to his father many years before, but that oath defined Hannibal, and they would soon find out the depth of his loyalty to it.

Hannibal wasted little time in attacking Saguntum, well aware that he was probably provoking the Second Punic War.

He laid siege to the city. His troops had hot oil poured on them by the defenders on the city walls. Hannibal led the attack on the most heavily fortified part of the city, where he was wounded in the leg. The walls of Saguntum eventually crumbled, and the Carthaginians flooded into the city. Many of the survivors threw themselves into raging fires rather than be captured. Hannibal divided the riches of the city among his troops and sent some back to Carthage. Victory was very rewarding, and Hannibal's reputation grew both among the soldiers and among the people of Carthage.

The Romans soon declared war on Carthage; the Second Punic War had begun. It would be the bloodiest war ever fought in the ancient world, and it would determine whether Rome or Carthage influenced the rest of human history.

CHAPTER

3

Marching to the Alps

THE ENORMOUS ARMY THAT HANNIBAL LED OUT OF NEW CARTHAGE IN May of 218 B.C. stretched for miles. Hannibal would have ridden near the head of the endless column, and at his side as he started out were his brothers Mago and Hanno. The Numidian cavalry were next in line, often darting out to show their skill on a horse and urging the troops on as they headed north to the first range of mountains, the Pyrenees. Their javelin points would have glittered in the sun.

CROSSING THE PYRENEES

From New Carthage, Hannibal and his army headed straight north, often along the coast of Spain and going inland when they needed to avoid obvious ambush points. The bright blue sea with white waves would have been on their right, and the red earth in hills and terraces to their left. Even though most of Spain was now ruled by the Carthaginians, the land just south of the Pyrenees was filled with hostile Celtic tribes that would not have been afraid of the enormous army. There is evidence that Hannibal encountered more resistance from these tribes than he planned for. In fact, the journey to the Pyrenees was several hundred miles, roughly a third of the entire trip to the gates of Rome. For many of these early miles, the army was harassed constantly.

Hannibal's scouts knew this land well, and they knew that the best place to cross the Pyrenees was through a pass called the Col de Perthus. This pass is only 2,300 feet high. Hannibal realized that the Celts might continue to harass the army, and he stationed in the Pyrenees a force of approximately 11,000 men under the command of his brother Hanno to block the pass after the army came through to protect their rear. Hannibal left little to chance.

Just after getting through the pass and into southern Gaul (now France), Hannibal began to receive word from his more loyal and experienced troops that some of the Spanish mercenaries were already having second thoughts about the trip to Italy. These mercenaries were tired of the attacks from the Celts, dreaded the much higher mountain climb of the Alps, and wanted to return home. Some were ready to lead a mutiny.

Many Carthaginian generals simply would have executed the rebellious troops. Many later generals did exactly that when their command was threatened. Hannibal was different. He called a meeting and said that he would send home some of the troops to protect New Carthage and their homeland. He selected the rebellious troops to go back. By doing so, he avoided a larger conflict and made it seem that all of this was part of a plan. The army that was left was loyal to him and solidified his leadership. He had done away with dissent in the most practical and bloodless way he knew how. He knew leadership involved psychology and perception, and he was now seen to be even more in charge. He made friends and allies where he would have made enemies.

MARCHING TO THE RHÔNE RIVER

The army that crossed the Pyrenees and was now headed to the Rhône River was a smaller group, comprising roughly 50,000 infantry and 9,000 cavalry. Casualties from the fights with the Celts, defections, the loss of the Spanish mercenaries, and leaving behind a rear guard had cut the original force almost in half. Yet, because a smaller army can move faster and needs less food, the force reduction was not all bad. As the army marched the 180 miles from the Pyrenees to the Rhône, it ate everything in its path. Whole fields would be stripped bare of fruit, corn, vegetables, and olives. The sick and the dead would be left behind with enormous amounts of broken equipment, human and animal waste, and garbage. A smaller army could live more lightly on the land, but even a small army left dead zones behind that must have looked like tornado paths.

Hannibal had learned a lesson, as he always did. This time, he would try to avoid fights with the local hostile tribes by negotiating with them. So, when he entered Gaul, between the Pyrenees and the Rhône, he sent his scouts out to tribal leaders and asked them to meet him at his camp. He told the tribal chiefs in Gaul that he was only passing through and did not want their lands. He gave them lavish gifts and bribed them with chests of gold. As a result, they agreed to leave his army alone. Hannibal was not so much afraid of the fights they could give him as he was afraid of the time he would lose. He needed to keep ahead of Roman expectations of where he was, and of the Alpine winter.

The Carthaginian army marched quickly through what is now southern France, keeping the Mediterranean on their right.

One of Hannibal's biggest challenges in his surprise attack included crossing the Rhône River on the way to Italy. Some of the elephants refused to cross the river on their own, and Hannibal's men constructed rafts to transport them.

Historians disagree on exactly when and where they met the Rhône River, but most think it was September and several miles from the sea, where it is still an intact river and not a series of tributaries (the Rhône divides much like the Mississippi River, into a series of smaller rivers in a delta). The most likely spot is near where the city of Arles is today. The river there is roughly a half-mile wide, not too deep, and not too fast; a large army could make it across. No archaeological evidence exists as to exactly where the army crossed.

Hannibal and his army bought hundreds of boats, canoes, and anything that would float from the Gauls. The tribes made money not only from the original negotiations but from selling everything the Carthaginians needed to cross a major river. The Gauls were only too happy to see the army leave their land; however, another tribe was waiting across the river, and they were not as friendly as the Gauls.

THE VIOLENT VOLCAE

One of the most warlike tribes in the ancient world was the Celtic tribe called the Volcae. One of their concentrations was in the Rhône Valley. When they saw Hannibal's army ready to cross the river, they formed an army of their own on the far side (the eastern side) to fight the Carthaginians. Hannibal offered to negotiate, as he had done successfully before, but the tribe's leaders did not accept and had little need for gold. The Volcae probably had not heard of the army's path of destruction through small villages, including the rapes and beatings of locals. They almost certainly did not know who Hannibal was, or what changes the next few years would bring as the giant powers of Rome and Carthage fought to the death near their homelands. Yet they did know how to defend their people and livestock—and they felt threatened.

The Volcae and tribes like them did not form large armies in an attempt to conquer territory. The tribes formed instead along family and village affiliations. Their goal in conflict was to capture food and equipment and, in the process, gain prestige and bragging rights over other tribes. They did not form lines of cavalry or infantry—rather, they organized raiding parties of 20 to 50 men and women. They could, however, form an "army" of a thousand or more people if threatened. Only much later would they develop into larger fighting units and help defeat Rome.

Hannibal had a problem. He needed to get tens of thousands of soldiers and civilians and thousands of horses across a river while a large enemy force waited on the other side to attack. As he always did, he solved the problem with creativity and intelligence. He sent a small force of men several miles up the river, under cover of dark, to cross the river at dawn. They inflated their leather pouches and used them as flotation aids as they crossed the river at a point where it flowed very rapidly. The "commando" group then came down the western edge of the river and hid in the woods behind the Volcae. It was not the first or last time Hannibal would use surprise and multiple

Worshipping the Carthaginian Gods

Hannibal was a religious man, as most Carthaginians were. In fact, his name means "mercy of Baal." Of course, Carthaginians did not worship one god; their most important gods were Baal, Tanit, and Eshmun. Baal appears to have been known as "Rider of the Clouds" and "Lord of the Earth." He was most similar to the Egyptian god Amun-Ra, an aggressive god and the one on whom most mortals depended to intervene and make a journey safe or a sick relative well. Some think that the Carthaginians often sacrificed their firstborn children to Baal, but there is disagreement among experts about this.

Tanit was a goddess who appeared on many Carthaginian coins. She was a goddess of good fortune, and her symbol was a pyramid, over which were a sun and a crescent moon. Her symbol is found on many graves. Some think she also required human sacrifice, but not as much as Baal.

Eshmun was the god of healing. For a soldier, the god of healing would be a powerful god, prayed to often. For a time, the Carthaginians fronts to attack. The next day, Hannibal sent up a smoke signal to his hiding men to let them know that he was starting the river crossing. The Volcae stood on the eastern side of the river and howled and shouted, as they always did before a big battle. They were crazed with anticipation. They knew the soldiers and horses would be tired from crossing the river, and they waited to slaughter them.

When Hannibal's hidden forces attacked them from behind, the Volcae never knew what hit them. Suddenly they were not the attackers, and they had to defend themselves from two directions. They were confused and panicked. Soon the rafts

adopted a new god: the Greek god of war, Ares. Ares appears on bronze Carthaginian coins made right around the period of the Second Punic War (218 B.C.).

The gods had to be worshipped in temples, which were usually built on prominent locations near the palaces of the nobles (convenient for worship). Temples had many people on staff—priests (clean shaven), singers, musicians, scribes, and more. The walls reverberated with the sounds of flutes and tambourines during special ceremonies. The temple often held funeral urns, containing the remains of the dead. Sometimes a special area for the dead was built, called a necropolis.

The Bible mentions a place called a tophet—or roasting place—used by the Canaanites, ancestors of the Carthaginians. Some experts who have excavated the Carthage Tophet suggest that humans were roasted there, along with animals. Others argue that only stillborn infants were burned there, or children who had died of natural causes. Some experts argue that the young dead were sacrificed to the gods for the protection of the living. There is no question that the temples and tophets, and religion itself, were central to the lives of most ancient people.

with horses and riders hit the shore, and Hannibal and his army quickly won the battle. The Volcae ran for their lives.

SHOCKING THE ROMANS

The Roman Senate assumed Hannibal was still in Spain and sent out a large force—led by Cornelius Scipio—to fight him there. Their ships left Rome and landed in late August near the Rhône delta to get supplies and to try to rid the army of the seasickness many of them felt. The soldiers had a difficult time traveling in large ships thrown about in Mediterranean storms. Scipio sent out a routine scouting party along the Rhône's western side and the surrounding area. As fate would have it, they ran into a scouting party of Hannibal's that was moving southeast away from the river to try to find the best spot to start crossing the Alps.

The two scouting parties fought viciously, with many casualties on both sides. The Carthaginians broke off the encounter and headed back to tell Hannibal that a Roman force was nearby. When Scipio's men told him that Hannibal's army was near, he could not believe what he was hearing. He and all of Rome had assumed that no army could march as far and as fast as Hannibal's had. Scipio must have reasoned very quickly that Hannibal intended to attack Rome from the land, and he was shocked.

When Hannibal heard that a large Roman force was only a few miles away, he must have been tempted to strike—if only out of revenge for the losses from the scouting party's battle. As always, he did not let his emotions get in the way. He reasoned that a major fight would delay him, and that he needed more than ever to get to Rome quickly, because Scipio would be sending word back to the city about the planned land attack.

Scipio then set out to attack Hannibal to delay the march over the Alps and give Rome more time. Yet, when he arrived at the place the Carthaginians were supposed to be, they had

Hannibal is known as one of the greatest military geniuses in history. His war tactics and maneuvers were so effective, Roman generals were forced to study and mimic Hannibal's strategies in order to defeat him.

already moved on; all Scipio saw were the smoldering remains of campfires. Scipio was jolted yet again. He knew then that Hannibal was a foe unlike any other Roman enemy. No one else could move so many soldiers so fast. Rome was in for the fight of its life.

HITTING THE WALL OF MOUNTAINS

Hannibal needed to alter his plan to cross the Alps because he knew Scipio was looking for him but would not follow him into the more difficult parts of the mountains. So, Hannibal marched his army north for four days, away from the easiest route through the Alps from the lower Rhône Valley, to a more difficult section farther north. The large army could march approximately 10 miles a day, so historians estimate they marched about 40 miles out of their way to avoid the Romans. Eventually, they came to the Alpes du Dauphiné, the foothills of the Alps. Exactly where the army entered the first Alpine gorge is subject to great debate, but again no clear archaeological evidence exists. Roman historians describe various mountain and river features, but modern historians are left to speculate.

What is clear is that Hannibal's army had a second crisis of confidence. Looming beyond the foothills were giant walls of snowcapped land, not quite visible, and stories rippled through the army about the certain death that awaited them in these higher mountains above 12,000 feet. The men had marched over 800 miles, climbed a mountain range, fought more tribes than they could count, and forded a dangerous river. A Roman army was now chasing them. They knew their surprise cover had been blown. To reassure them, Hannibal gave one of his most moving speeches at exactly the moment his worried and weary troops most needed it.

> What sudden panic is this that has suddenly entered your hearts, where fear was never found before. You followed

me from Spain bent upon destroying Rome and setting the world free. Now, when you have already completed the greater distance, when you have made your way over the passes of the Pyrenees . . . tamed the violence of the mighty Rhône and crossed its waters in the face of countless Gallic warriors, when you have the Alps nearly in sight and know that on the other side is Italy, now at the very doors of the enemy you stop!

What do you think the Alps are? They are nothing more than high mountains. No part of the earth touches the sky there. . . . Common men live in the Alps, they till the soil, they herd their animals there. . . . Steel your hearts, march forward and halt only when you have scaled the walls of Rome.

The speech worked; the men continued onward and upward. Hannibal had a way of communicating with his troops at just the right time with just the right information. Rumors did not have a chance to overwhelm the troops. They trusted him, and they knew they were much less of a force without him.

The best way to climb the Alps when moving from west to east is to find the small valleys that cut through the mountains and then to find the lowest pass above the valley. These transverse valleys usually contain small rivers, which begin as streams high in the mountains. The water can be life giving and sustain an army, but it can also be life threatening when mountain rains create treacherous footing, small floods, and mudslides.

The Alps rise gradually from their foothills, and the army found itself in higher and more dangerous terrain with every mile. The rocks became larger and harder to get around, the paths were narrower and steeper, and surrounding cliffs appeared more menacing. The most frightening aspect of the cliffs soon became the people who stood on them, staring down at the army.

FIGHTING THE ALLOBROGES

It was Hannibal's fate to meet not one but two of the most warlike local tribes on this part of the journey. He had out-maneuvered and defeated the Volcae at the Rhône and now confronted a related tribe called the Allobroges who controlled many of the passes leading into Italy. Their largest village was near where modern-day Grenoble is, and they became one of Rome's bitterest enemies many years later. In 218 B.C., they were a formidable foe, and Hannibal was marching right through their domain.

At first, the Allobroge scouts tried to conceal themselves. As the army made its way to higher and narrower gorges, how-ever, the growing number of Allobroges did not bother to hide. They watched from above, and Hannibal became more and more restless about the possibility of ambush. His army column was now only one person or animal wide in most places. The drop to the river below was a long one, and the trails were nar-row and steep. Some of the men became spooked by the figures moving quickly above them along the ledges. Rumors started among the troops that some were missing after they went look-ing for firewood.

Hannibal always relied on scouts for information. One day, soon after entering the mountains, he sent a team of his best to spy on the Allobroges. One scout overheard some tribe mem-bers saying they would return to their village that night. Han-nibal seized the opportunity and sent a small force higher up into the mountains as night fell, much as he had done against the Volcae when he sent a small force upriver to get behind the enemy. When dawn broke the next day, some of Hanni-bal's men were looking down on the men who were looking down on the main army. Hannibal had set a trap. Scholars dis-agree on whether the Allobroges knew that their ambush was being ambushed, but they attacked the main army below them for the first time—suddenly screaming war cries that echoed throughout the narrow valley below, pushing boulders down, shooting arrows at both men and horses, and slinging rocks of all sizes. The tribes deliberately shot the horses to make them rear up and lose their footing and fall into the gorge. The falling horses took their riders and other animals they were tied to with them. Some pack animals panicked and rushed upward, knocking more men and animals off the path into the gorge below.

The Allobroges then rushed down the steep gorge face to continue the attack. Hannibal and his small force above the Allobroges waited, and then they literally jumped into the action when they could wait no longer. The fighting was confused, vicious, and devastating. In hand-to-hand combat, the Allobroges were no match for the heavily armed Carthaginian professional fighters, and soon the tribesmen were soundly defeated. The survivors ran higher into the mountains. Many Carthaginian soldiers had lost their lives, or their supplies and animals, and as they continued marching through the next mountain pass there was almost complete silence as the men thought of what they had seen.

Word of the battle spread quickly through the neighboring Alpine valleys to other tribes. Fear of Hannibal and his men spread just as rapidly. Few would dare attack them now, and the march went faster. Finally, the lower Alps had been crossed. It was late September, and the highest mountains were now visible. The worst was yet to come.

Slashing into Italy

THE ALPS THAT NOW TOWERED BEFORE HANNIBAL AND HIS TROOPS WERE
roughly 13,000 feet high, more than twice the height of the
lower Alps they had just come through. These new peaks were
often cloud covered, which may have helped diminish the fear
of what was about to happen. At some point, however, a cloud-
less day would have dawned, and the army must have been in
awe of the giants in front of them.

The army had now been in the mountains more than a week,
and they stopped to rest and make camp in one of the high valleys. They had been through an ordeal, and Hannibal was smart
enough to know when to let his troops rest. They would need
their strength for mountain climbing.

TRAPPED BY THE MOUNTAIN PEOPLE

Hannibal and his men must have been surprised when they first saw a group of men approach their camp from the direction of the highest mountains. The men were carrying branches shaped into wreaths as symbols of peace. There were a group of elders from a series of mountain villages, sent to make peace with this foreign army, certainly the largest they had ever seen. They told Hannibal that they had heard about his victory over the Allobroges, and they had learned from it. They would not want to attack such a great force, and, as a show of good will, they would provide guides through these highest peaks.

Who were these mountain people? The Greek historian Diodorus wrote about them in the first century B.C.:

> Here in this rough country, men and women live a toilsome and luckless life. . . . They hunt and trap wild animals and drink only water and milk. Most of their diet consists of meager vegetables which they cultivate in some plots on the stony ground and the flesh of the animals they hunt. They have no wheat or vineyards. They live either in huts with their cattle, or in hollow rocks and caves, yet they possess the strength and courage of wild beasts.

The Roman historian Pliny the Elder wrote that many of these mountain people had goiter, a disease caused by a lack of iodine and other nutrients that disfigures people. The mountain people tended to live in fortified villages, had very simple lives, and were as distrustful of strangers as any other tribe might be. Hannibal doubted the sincerity of their offer of guides, but he accepted it anyway. He had plenty of scouts but few guides. The latter knew the local terrain.

Hannibal was right to be wary. The guides led his troops to one of the most dangerous and narrow gaps in the higher

Alps, where the mountain tribes had banded together to get rid of this enemy. Hannibal must have known the trap he was walking into, but he realized it too late to turn around. The mountain tribes ambushed Hannibal's army in much the same way as the Allobroges did. Their war cries came an instant before large boulders began raining down on the column of Hannibal's soldiers and animals. This time, there was no upper ledge from which Hannibal could conduct a surprise attack. This enemy had learned about Hannibal's tactics and thought they could defeat him and take all the wealth his army was carrying. This time, he could do nothing but force his army to fight through the narrow pass to the broader ground on the other side. Tons of rock came crashing down on the column, and thousand of arrows and spears wounded and killed both men and animals. The river below ran red with blood and bodies.

As always, Hannibal had learned from the previous fight. He learned that the elephants were more valuable at the head of the column, so if they panicked—as they would—they would not trample anyone but the enemy in front of them. The elephants ran through the narrow gorge in a fury, trampling the mountain people who tried to block the exit of the pass. Hannibal had learned that the best way to survive was to move as quickly as possible through the eye of the needle. To be trapped in the pass was to die. There was no room to turn around and retreat. Therefore, his forces were told to keep moving at any cost, even if it meant throwing dead bodies—and even injured ones—down into the gorge. Some of the dead were used as shields to help stop the barrage of rocks and arrows. At several points, Hannibal dismounted and fought the tribesmen hand to hand. He urged his men to keep moving, to not stop for anything. The Carthaginians did not believe in the more modern tactic of leaving no man behind. They left many.

The mountain people had no Hannibal. They could do no more than vanish when their attack was unsuccessful after

While climbing the Alps was an enormous feat, descending these treacherous mountains proved fatal to almost half of Hannibal's forces. Icy conditions, blocked paths, and steep ledges caused many Carthaginian soldiers to stumble or slip off the side of the mountains.

hours of intense fighting. The Carthaginians and their elephants had broken through the last enemy barriers and kept going into the valley beyond. When Hannibal's army finally broke through, the mountain people could only watch from whatever hiding place they had. They knew that they could double back into the gorge later and loot, kill, and capture anyone and anything left in the pass. They would torture many of the survivors, to vent their rage against this enormous enemy who seemed so organized, determined, and well armed.

Infantry Versus Cavalry

Soldiers on horses versus soldiers on foot—many ancient battles came down to that confrontation. The Greeks had developed infantry (soldiers on foot) arms and tactics for hundreds of years in the ancient world, as city-state warred with city-state on hilly terrain that was unsuited for the chariots used in the ancient Near East. The Greeks invented the phalanx, a close grouping of soldiers (usually eight rows deep) that created walls of men more difficult to fight than individual men. The Greeks used longer spears (called *sarissas*, which measured about 18 feet long) than had been used before, making their infantry even harder to fight.

Yet the breeding of horses for size and strength continued throughout the ancient world, and eventually horses became big and strong enough to carry fully armored soldiers on their backs. People who lived in areas where it was hard to farm relied on raising cattle and became expert riders as soon as they could walk. Cavalry (warriors on horses) became an innovation that spread throughout the ancient world from Eurasia. In the fourth century B.C., Philip II of Macedon and his son, Alexander the Great, combined Greek infantry tactics with cavalry and were unbeatable. Combinations of infantry and cavalry became the norm. At first, cavalries only supported the infantry. Eventually the roles switched, and infantries supported the main fighting force—the cavalry. A skilled archer or javelin thrower on horseback became the most feared warrior in the ancient world. After the Punic Wars with Carthage, Rome wanted to make sure that the infantry and cavalry could both move quickly to where they were needed. Thus, the Romans built roads that have lasted to this day.

DEFEATING THE WORST ENEMIES YET

The army had been ambushed twice in the past few days and needed to regroup on the other side of the mountain they had just climbed. The men cleared the snow from a large area and set up tents and campfires. Now, new enemies attacked them: It was cold, the mountain winds were brutal, and so many pack animals had been lost that supplies were running very low. At first, only the badly wounded died from cold and starvation. Soon, the healthy were dying as well. Some of the animals were slaughtered for food. The morale of the troops was as low as it had ever been, or ever would be.

Hannibal had an instinct for when he needed to provide inspiration. At dawn following the day of the second ambush, he climbed several hundred feet to the top of the nearest mountain ridge, probably the Col de la Traversette. He looked down at Italy. He saw the foothills of the Alps stretching into the rich and green Po Valley. He came back to camp and told his men about what he had seen. They were almost there. The worst was over. As always, the soldiers took heart when they heard their leader's message. They believed.

What no one knew was that the forces of geology and gravity were against them. The eastern slopes of the Alps, the Italian side, are much steeper than the western side. As the scouts marked a track down the mountains, the column followed. The track was covered in snow, and even a slight stumble would push man or beast into a free fall down the mountain. The footing became worse as the men and animals tramped it into a hard and slick surface. The eastern side of the mountains would thaw in the morning and then freeze again when the sun went behind the mountains after noon. The gorge below was thousands of feet deep, and many of the soldiers slid right to the edge of the narrow path and grabbed for anything that could stop them. Their packs were heavy, and they were weak from hunger. Often, nothing stopped them from slipping over the edge and falling to certain death. Some of the men who were able to grab something had to give up after dangling over the edge, and allowed themselves to fall into the gorges below. They were too weak and too cold to hang on for very long. They experienced one mountain-climbing accident after another, a cascade of personal disasters.

Suddenly, the scouts came to a place on a ledge where the path had been destroyed by a recent landslide. Hannibal and his engineers had to make a decision—go back up the mountain and find a new path or rebuild and widen the previous path. They chose the second way, but soon it became clear that an enormous boulder blocked them. The boulder was impossible to move and larger than a modern two-story house. Instead, the engineers took advantage of the wisdom of the farmers in the army. For centuries, farmers had cleared their land of large rocks by building a fire under them and pouring cold water or old wine on the heated rocks, which caused them to crack. The men built an enormous fire around the rock, fed by wood passed along the ledge by other soldiers. The flames leaped high against the mountain, and soon the rock began to glow a dull red at its base. Hannibal gave the order at just the right moment, and his men poured wineskins filled with sour wine (essentially vinegar) on it, creating several cracks. They then went to work with picks and axes, and after four days the enormous boulder became several pieces of rock that were pushed down into the gorge or used to help rebuild the path.

Slowly, rock by rock, the army descended. The last to get down were the elephants. Historians say that the army lost more men coming down the steep Italian side of the Alps than they lost fighting the tribe or mountain people. The army that crossed the Rhône was roughly 45,000 strong. Coming down out of the mountains, the army had only 26,000 men left. The survivors looked more like animals than men. They were weak, starving, and freezing—an army of dead men walking and riding.

As the soldiers finally rode and marched out of the high mountain into the low foothills, they collapsed. The unwounded

The Roman Legion

The Roman army that fought Hannibal was composed of legions. These legions were models of organization, efficiency, and clarity of purpose. They became a military model for centuries following the Second Punic War. Each legion had a commander and roughly 60 centurions to enforce the carrying out of orders. Each legion also had between 4,500 and 6,000 men, drawn from all parts of Italy. Men who didn't know one another were more likely to listen to their leaders and not form mutinous bands. Most of the Roman soldiers in the republic phase were farmers who had at least a small plot of land and joined the army for a period of time during crisis. The Roman Empire often was in crisis in its early years.

The core of each legion was the heavily armed infantry, who were divided into units—called maniples—of 300 to 400 men. Each maniple had three subunits. These were called lines, and each line had a different role in battle. The first line was for charging the enemy and trying to break the enemy's ranks. These were the youngest, and usually the most fearless, men. Many were new recruits. They usually did not know the horrors of war, so they were eager to fight. The second line included more experienced soldiers and was used to strike at the enemy when the first line tired or was defeated. The third line was the most expert, skilled, and battle tested. They only entered the battle if needed.

The average soldier routinely carried about 70 pounds of equipment and weaponry and was expected to be able to walk at a pace of more than four miles per hour for at least five hours per day. Most legion soldiers had a small dagger (*puglio*), a short sword about two feet long (*gladius*), a spear (*hasta* or *pilum*), and a shield (*scutum*). They were protected by scaled armor that was thick and heavy. Their main tactic was never to engage an enemy soldier in a sword fight. The goal was to knock the hand-to-hand opponent off balance with the shield and then use the dagger or sword to kill.

horses carried two and three riders, and the wounded ones were led by the surviving pack animals. As soon as the soldiers set up a large base camp, they let the surviving animals graze on the lush grasses of the Italian countryside. The animals were mad with hunger, and they devoured whatever they could. Gradually, man and beast began to regain their strength. The elephants were near death, but none had died.

FIRST ROMAN BLOOD

Hannibal and his army came out of the mountains into the Po Valley, probably west of the modern city of Turin. He knew his army desperately needed rest and food, but they could not rest for too long. Soon, his scouts reported that Scipio was headed north to the Po Valley from Rome with an army. Scipio had not had time to train some of his soldiers, in his rush to battle Hannibal as far away from Rome as possible. Scipio no doubt thought that most of Hannibal's army would have died in the mountains, and he may not have believed he would need a large and expert force to defeat what was left.

The first battle loomed as both armies maneuvered into position. They both arrived at the Ticinus River, a tributary of the Po River, and each side prepared for the all-important first battle. Ancient historians report that each commander gave an impassioned speech before the battle. Hannibal told his men that the Alps were now behind them and there was no going back. Retreat was not an option. They were now in enemy territory, isolated and alone. Their survival depended on their courage and skill, and nothing else. Rome lay ahead, and each man would get enough gold, silver, and women that he would live like a king. To those who fought hardest, he would award tax-free land in Italy, Africa, or Spain.

Scipio gave his speech, as well. He told his men that they would face "ghosts and the mere shadows of men" who had been defeated by the Alps. The enemy was "riding lame animals"

The series of Punic Wars marked a change in war strategy. Rome was forced to adapt to Carthage's military tactics and invent weapons, while Hannibal revolutionized infantry formations and initiated one of the most famous surprise attacks in history.

and "fighting with broken weapons." They would be no match for Roman legions. Hannibal was "a young upstart and criminal, drunk with ambition." These enemies were in their land and wanted the lives of their wives and children—they must be stopped.

Scipio made the first move. His men charged across the river and into an open plain. Hannibal's tactics were to rely on the Numidian cavalry to devastate the charge and go right after Scipio. It was no contest. The Numidian riders were so fast and skillful that the Roman legions were caught off guard and pushed back into the river. Scipio was surrounded and about to be killed when his 17-year-old son, also named Scipio, rode full gallop to his father's rescue and carried him away, seriously wounded. The younger Scipio would become a legendary leader later, but on this day he was just trying to save his father. The Roman troops were in shock and ran back to the walled city of Placentia. The Carthaginians celebrated their first victory.

Shock and Awe in Italy

THE ROMANS ALWAYS HAD MORE CITIZEN-SOLDIERS ON HAND TO TAKE THE place of the dead and injured. Commander Sempronius Longus quickly brought his large army north to join what was left of Scipio's. He arrived at Placentia eager to fight Hannibal. If he could defeat Hannibal where Scipio had failed, Rome would reward him with fame and glory. He could prove his superiority to all other commanders, both Roman and Carthaginian. The stakes were high. He did not listen to Scipio, who told him to be wary of this Carthaginian general whose men seemed to fight with lightning quickness and without fear. Scipio advised Sempronius to wait and let winter do its work to help starve the enemy. The Romans could be secure in winter quarters, do more training and planning, and hunt down the Carthaginians in the spring. It was a good plan.

Sempronius hated the idea of delaying. He wanted to be a heroic leader, and waiting seemed like cowardice. He knew he had numerical superiority, with approximately 40,000 men against Hannibal's less than 30,000. With Scipio injured, he took control of both armies and planned for an immediate battle.

VICTORY AT TREBBIA

Hannibal, on the other hand, did not let his emotions or ambitions get the better of him. He knew that he had an advantage in an open plain, based on what he saw at Ticinus. He also wanted to have a second advantage: surprise. If he could find an area near Placentia that would allow him to hide some soldiers and Numidian cavalry, he could have surprise working in his favor. He and his scouts found an ideal area near the Trebbia River, also a tributary of the Po, with shrubs and undergrowth that could hide men if an enemy were not looking for them. Horses and even elephants had been trained to lie down and be covered with anything to conceal them. Rome did know Hannibal's tactics yet and still underestimated him.

The most common battle plan during the Second Punic War era was to attack an enemy's front lines of infantry with archers who were safely behind their own infantry. Then the infantry would advance on the enemy, keeping the cavalry to the sides, or flanks. When the infantries were fully engaged, the cavalry would sweep in from the sides and make deadly attacks, often keeping the opposing infantry from fleeing. Timing and skill were everything, at least the way Hannibal fought. He did not believe in simply bludgeoning the opponent to death. He believed in having a tactical advantage. He wanted to outsmart his opponent, and he did.

As soon as one infantry unit started to panic and run, others would get caught up in that panic. A rout usually followed, with many soldiers either escaping or being slaughtered. Hannibal was a master at varying the common battle plan. He was also a master at not giving up. Many battles ended when a commander was killed or decided to escape with his bodyguards. Troops without a leader often do not continue to fight—the ultimate testimony to the importance of leadership. Hannibal never fled a battle, at least not while he was fighting in Italy.

Hannibal needed a way to get Sempronius to come out into the open plains near the Trebbia. He sent a group of Numidians to the Roman camp at dawn on a cold and snowy morning in December of 218 B.C. to taunt the Romans. When Sempronius heard the taunts, he lost control of himself and ordered his troops into the field. The Numidians carried out their plan. They pretended to be frightened, and they retreated farther and farther away from the fortified Roman camp near Placentia. Sempronius tasted complete victory and ordered his entire army into battle. Fortune and glory would be his. Scipio, wounded in his tent, sensed something was wrong with this seemingly easy victory and tried to warn Sempronius. The new commander did not listen. His arrogance and ambition would kill many soldiers that day.

Suddenly, the Numidian cavalry stopped retreating and turned around to face the charging Romans. The Carthaginian elephants and thousands of the soldiers joined them. The two armies became opposing tidal waves of bodies, swords, spears, horses, and elephants that crashed into each other with an enormous roar. At first, the battle was a standoff, with neither side winning. The white snow on the ground melted into red as warm blood was spilled everywhere. Soon, Hannibal signaled for the surprise attack. At first, the Romans didn't notice the Carthaginian soldiers coming out of hiding to charge them from behind. When they felt the second attacking wave, they did something very few later Roman armies would do: They panicked. They lashed out without control, and their lines caved in. They were under attack from all sides. Soon, there were no

Although outnumbered, Hannibal's forces overwhelmed Roman legions continuously throughout the Second Punic War. It was only when Roman generals used his own tactics against Hannibal that the tide of fortune began to change for both civilizations.

lines—only individual Roman men fighting for survival and then running for their lives.

Hannibal and his outnumbered army had won a decisive and now legendary battle. He had used psychology and surprise tactics to defeat his opponent, keeping his emotions in check while others lost theirs. Scipio and Sempronius now knew that they faced an opposing general who had the courage and cunning not seen since Alexander the Great nearly 150 years earlier. The two Romans led their survivors to a large fortified camp in the town of Cremona, and then Sempronius left for Rome to try to explain to the Roman Senate and people why he had lost. He was humiliated and would not be heard from again in Roman history.

BRILLIANCE AT LAKE TRASIMENE

Hannibal and his men settled into northern Italy for a long and bitter winter. They raided villages for food and shelter, and they terrified residents who came into contact or even had heard of the enemy army marching toward Rome. Winter took its toll on the army, however—all but one of the elephants died. They had survived the trip over the Alps but were not able to find enough food to avoid starvation during the long winter months. Fevers spread through the army as well, blinding some and killing others.

The Roman Senate now committed 10 legions to the fight against Hannibal but agreed to wait until spring. Flaminius replaced Sempronius and marched his army north to try to block the road to Rome. Servilius took another large Roman army and marched around the Apennine Mountains to protect the eastern half of Italy. Hannibal seemed to the Romans to have only one goal at this point: to get to Rome as fast as possible. He marched his men due south as soon as the spring of 217 B.C. allowed. He raced past Flaminius and his army, who now pursued him.

Hannibal remembered the devastating attacks on his army in the mountains; as he rode into central Italy near Lake Trasimene, he noticed a perfect spot for an ambush of the kind he had endured months earlier. A narrow and level plain was bound by steep cliffs on one side and by the lake on the other. The road narrowed at the base of the high hills. Hannibal slowed down his army and made Flaminius think he was tiring. Hannibal placed his men at each end of the plain and in the hills above. Flaminius entered the narrowed plain near the lake on a morning in June of 217 B.C., sure that he was getting close to attacking Hannibal and becoming a Roman hero himself. He was clueless. A heavy mist hid Hannibal's three-pronged attack. The trap was sprung, and the attack came so quickly that some of the Roman soldiers could not even raise their weapons. Flaminius, as arrogant and impulsive as Sempronius had been, was killed, and his armor was carried away as a prize. Many Romans drowned in the lake as they fled, brought under by their heavy armor and weapons. No one even noticed that the area was struck that day by a major earthquake; Romans now thought of Hannibal as a much greater disaster than anything nature could devise. They now knew he was a brilliant field commander.

The citizens of Rome were devastated by the news of the defeat at Lake Trasimene. Wives and mothers of soldiers waited inside the gates of Rome, looking at every returning soldier to see if their husband or son had survived. The women pressed the surviving soldiers and other stragglers for news. City magistrate Marcus Pomponius came forth from the senate and announced, "We have been beaten in a great battle." With those words, he turned his back on the crowd and retreated to the safety of the senate.

THE GREATEST VICTORY, THE GREATEST DEFEAT: CANNAE

The Roman Senate was now deeply divided on how to battle Hannibal. One group, led by Quintus Fabius Maximus, the head of Rome, wanted to do nothing but fortify Rome and make it too expensive for Hannibal to attack the city. This group did not want to fight Hannibal directly. They advocated being patient and letting time take its toll on an army so far away from home. An opposing group, led by consuls Lucius Aemilius Paullus and C. Terentius Varro, wanted to force a decisive final confrontation with Hannibal, putting all their forces together and overwhelming their opponent with shock and awe. Soon, the senate decided that Paullus and Varro were right. Caution was not the answer. Spectacular displays of Roman military would win the day.

Meanwhile, Hannibal did not head directly for Rome but instead went looking for both allies and food. Hannibal had

The Cannae Model

The Battle of Cannae is famous for many reasons, but mostly as a model of the perfect battle. The arrangement of forces before the battle, their movements during the battle, and the decisive importance of the outcome have military historians studying it even now. Many have noted that the outcome of a battle is often determined before the battle even begins. Hannibal had placed his soldiers where they could do the most good. He had planned for signals that allowed a choreography of movement during the battle, especially the pincer movement that trapped the Romans. Encircling an entire army by attacking not only the front lines but both flanks at the same time became an ideal that many ancient and modern military commanders have strived to attain.

Frederick the Great, General Dwight Eisenhower, and General Norman Schwarzkopf are only three examples of leaders who used the Cannae model as they prepared for a battle. When Iraqi troops were surrounded and routed in the 1991 Gulf War by Schwarzkopf's Coalition Forces, history was repeating itself. The only problem with the Cannae model is that the battle did not win the war. The Romans did not give up after the greatest military defeat in ancient times. Instead, they became more determined than ever.

reasoned that, as he defeated Rome in battle after battle, Italian cities would abandon their alliances with Rome and come over to his side. He knew that he needed more men—with each battle, the Romans had thrown more forces at him, and this pattern of attack would be repeated. He knew that he did not yet have enough battering rams, catapults, and other siege equipment to assault Rome. He also reasoned that he needed to get to the richest farmlands and make sure he could feed his army. The closer he got to Rome, the fewer farms he found, so he veered toward the Adriatic Coast in southeastern Italy, which had some of Italy's richest wheat fields. In the spring of 216 B.C., he established a camp in the region known as Apulia, at the city of Cannae. Hannibal found a ruined fort that was surrounded by ripening crops of all kinds, especially summer wheat. He fattened his army with some new soldiers, and he fattened his soldiers with some of the most abundant food in the ancient world.

Paullus and Varro arrived at Cannae in late July of 216 B.C. They had more than 80,000 well-trained soldiers, along with an unusual power-sharing arrangement. One would take command of the army on odd-numbered days, and the other on even-numbered days. On August 2, Varro was in command; he ordered his men to advance on Hannibal's men, who were stationed on the plains around Cannae. Their overwhelming numbers would push through any army that Hannibal could throw at them. Hannibal's army was roughly half their size.

As always, Hannibal had the superior battle plan. He would let the Roman army pierce his front lines and think they were winning the battle. He would let the Romans advance but push them closer and closer together and then surround them. The speed of the Numidian cavalry enabled him to do just that. Hannibal had stationed the cavalry on either side of the main battle, and they worked their way in toward the center. Much of the Roman infantry were tightly packed into a confined space in the middle of the plain, making it hard to even use their weapons. The Numidians and other cavalry troops attacked them from all

Lucius Aemilius Paullus pushed for a face-to-face confrontation with Hannibal and was crushed by Hannibal's smaller forces. Paullus lost most of his troops and was killed, inciting doubt and fear in Rome and its citizens.

sides and closed in toward the center, peeling away layer after layer of Roman soldiers. The only survivors were those who ran for their lives.

Hannibal always seemed to have some natural force on his side in a crucial battle. This day, the sun and wind helped blind the Roman troops as they marched east. Any advantage in battle can help, and—just as the mists at Lake Trasimene helped disguise Hannibal's attack—now the elements again favored the Carthaginians. Of course, the battle stories are told only by Roman historians, so excuses for defeat are easy to find.

Roman losses have been estimated at 50,000 men, the largest in their history in a single battle. Historians have said that Cannae was the deadliest day in world combat history until the Battle of Somme in 1916. Hannibal had developed the better battle plan, and he was opposed by two generals who shared decision-making and thus lost control. Cannae is studied to this day by people who want to learn more about the history of warfare. Many highly educated commanders throughout the modern world know the battle by heart. Cannae is the model for a battle of annihilation, of complete domination of an opponent. Hannibal became a legend that day, and Rome would never fight him again in a large battle. The year 216 B.C. would mark the high point of Hannibal's war on Rome.

When Romans heard about the defeat at Cannae, many lost their minds. Some packed up and left Rome for good. Some flocked to temples and asked the priests for guidance. In Rome's central marketplace, human sacrifices began, in an effort to appease the gods and stop the Carthaginian war machine. First, a man and a woman from Gaul were killed. Then a couple from Greece was sacrificed. Roman citizens waited to see if the sacrifices would work. All 16-year-old boys were drafted into the Roman legions. Many criminals were let out of prisons and made part of the Roman defense. Women were forbidden to mourn in public and were ordered to remain in their homes. The gates of the city were closely guarded so that no one could escape. All public meetings were suspended. Romans waited for certain death and enslavement.

CHAPTER

6

A War Without Victory

THE ROMAN ARMY WAS DESTROYED AT CANNAE, AND HANNIBAL'S ARMY now had a clear path to Rome. He was a four-day march away from total victory, and his officers urged him to march immediately to Rome. Hannibal hesitated. One officer angrily said, "You know how to win a battle, Hannibal, but not how to use one." They had won every battle against Roman legions, and now the army could go wherever it wanted. Nothing could stop it except Hannibal himself. Hannibal did not march on Rome, and, as a result, the Roman Republic was saved. When the city finally stopped panicking, the Roman Senate stepped in with some much-needed leadership. Fabius was now looked to as a wise man. His strategy of patience, and not confrontation, was adopted; as a result, a long war of attrition began. Fabius assumed more and more power over both government and the military, and he came to be known as Fabius "the Delayer." Such a title is not a glorious one, but "the Delayer" proved effective over the long run.

Historians disagree on why Hannibal did not attack Rome after Cannae. Some think he felt that he could not afford a long siege, which would keep his army in one place too long and make it vulnerable. The walls of Rome were extremely high and thick, and tall towers would have to be built to crack the outer and inner walls. Some think that Hannibal was growing weary of battle and even sickened by the sight of so much bloodshed at Cannae. He could not rouse himself or his men to move quickly into battle again. He may have believed he had proven something, and marching on Rome was not needed. He said, "I am not carrying on a war of extermination against the Romans. I am contending for honor." He may have felt that the battle for honor was won.

Others think Hannibal assumed that the plan to have many of the Italian cities come over to his side would now take effect, and, in fact, many cities did declare themselves free from Rome. Many villages and cities in the provinces of Apulia, Campania, and Lucania supported the Carthaginians. Hannibal's plan was working, but it was a flawed plan. Just enough cities remained loyal to Rome that Hannibal would never acquire enough men and supplies to take over all of Italy. Too many villages had family members in the Roman army, or businesses that had been successful dealing with Rome. Too many people were loyal to their own kind. The Carthaginian army, to them, was an occupying force on their land and would never be welcome.

HANNIBAL IS STALEMATED

Hannibal decided that, rather than attack Rome, he would march his army to the southern coast of Italy on the Mediterranean side and gain control of a port city there. He would then be able to send messages to and from Carthage and receive supplies and replacement soldiers. He sent a part of his army on to the city of Naples, but its citizens proved surprisingly strong and resilient, and a siege of that city did not work. Hannibal as a leader was brilliant in battle, but he did not have the patience for a long siege. His tactics were bold and innovative, not suited for traditional waiting games.

Hannibal then marched north approximately 16 miles and did not encounter as much resistance at the city of Capua. This was Italy's second or third largest city during this time, and it was famous for its wine, wealth, and luxuries. Hannibal captured it and settled in. His soldiers found many pleasures and rewards in Capua, and some have suggested that the army softened and lost its will to fight. Hannibal must have seen this stay as one of the rewards of victory.

Fabius came up with a tactic that we now call the "scorched earth" plan. He knew he could not defeat Hannibal in a direct confrontation, but he could try to weaken the Carthaginian army by making it harder for them to get food. Fabius ordered that all corn and wheat in the area around Capua were to be cut down and put in vast storage facilities guarded by Roman legions. No corn was to be left standing, and selling supplies to the enemy was against the law. Hannibal's army then had to spend a good deal of effort conquering areas near Capua to capture food. He would eventually have to move his army back to the Apulia region on the Adriatic coast to ensure enough food. Wherever Hannibal's army went, the Roman armies followed, watched, and never attacked.

Fabius was also helped when his officers decided they would refuse to accept pay. When some officers showed their Roman patriotism this way, others followed. The Roman economy had suffered after the defeat at Cannae, and property taxes had to be increased to help raise a new army. The officer corps raised Roman morale with their gesture.

THE LAKE OF THE DEAD

Hannibal spoke Greek fluently and would have known many parts of Homer's *Odyssey* by heart. Hannibal and his army were becoming warrior-wanderers in 215 and 214 B.C. Hannibal must have thought about Odysseus, the legendary warrior-wanderer who was also away from his wife and son for years on end. There is a scene in the *Odyssey* where Odysseus descends to Hades and meets the souls of men slain in battle. The entrance to the underworld was, according to Greek and Roman tradition, Lake Avernus (now Averno). This is a volcanic crater lake in extreme southern Italy, approximately a mile wide and more than 200 feet deep. The name *Avernus* means "birdless"; the vapors of the volcano may have kept birds away, at least according to the legend.

Hannibal was a religious man, and his religion must have included some of these ancient beliefs about Lake Avernus. The realm of the dead came nearest to the living here. Offerings paid to the gods of the dead would be accepted. The Elysian Fields were here, as was the grotto of the prophetess Sibyl. This was sacred ground for an ancient warrior.

Hannibal had to see Lake Avernus. He took a few of his men and slashed through the thick woods to the shore of the lake. He must have been deeply moved, knowing that—according to his religion—the souls of dead soldiers were just below. He had seen many dead soldiers. He was responsible for their deaths. He almost certainly made a sacrifice at a temple on the shores.

STEALING TARENTUM

Soon after visiting Lake Avernus, Hannibal was approached by five citizens of the city of Tarentum. The city was near the lake and on the very southern coast of Italy. It had a large harbor and was a well-fortified port under Roman control. A large Roman garrison defended the city. Hannibal realized that capturing this port would be a prize, especially because he had not been able to capture the port city of Naples. He needed more communication with Carthage, more supplies, and more soldiers. He needed to control one of these ports, and Capua was not ideal for that.

The citizens told Hannibal that they were sympathetic to his cause and wanted freedom from Rome. Hannibal listened carefully and began to hatch a plan that would take a year to develop. He told the citizens they would have their chance to be free from Rome, but they needed to be patient. Hannibal returned to the region of Apulia for the winter of 214–213 B.C. That winter, several historians think Hannibal fell in love with a beautiful young woman from the surrounding countryside. He had been away from his wife and child for five years and received only sporadic news about them. He was a powerful and handsome young man who must have attracted many women. He apparently let his guard down at least once. The Roman writer Lucian later created a story in which Alexander the Great meets Hannibal in the underworld and berates him for falling in love and allowing a woman to captivate him. In the story, Alexander accuses Hannibal of neglecting his troops and his military duties. Hannibal had not been in a major battle since Cannae, two years earlier. Something was distracting him from full-time war making.

In the spring of 213 B.C., Hannibal, in love or not, left Apulia and marched his army to the city of Tarentum. Hannibal had hatched a plot to conquer the city without a long siege, for which he had neither the equipment nor the patience. He knew that some of the citizens in Tarentum wanted to be free of Rome. Hannibal arranged to meet secretly with two of them. They agreed that, if some of Hannibal's men could be let in through the gates to the city under the cover of night, they could take the city before the Roman soldiers knew what happened. The heavy gates were bolted and barred during the night, and no one was

As he left Carthage and its queen, Dido, Aeneas saw a plume of black smoke rise from the city, not knowing it was Dido's funeral pyre burning after she had killed herself from the despair of losing him. Dido's curse on Rome provided the mythological foundation for war between the two civilizations, only to be resolved at the end of the Punic Wars.

allowed in or out of the city. That would be the best time for a commando raid. Hannibal would spare the citizens of Tarentum and only attack the Romans living among them.

Hannibal and his insiders waited for a moonless night. They waited until there were no sounds within the city, and then a small signal fire was lit by some of Hannibal's men who were stationed near the gate, on the outside. The conspirators inside saw the signal fire and made their move. They jumped the Roman sentries who were guarding the high walls and watchtowers. Then they hacked through the heavy wooden bars that bolted the door shut and swung open the gates. The Carthaginians were right there, and they poured into the city. They had planned it so that some of the cavalry rode through a second gate that had just been swung open. Their timing was perfect. They quietly advanced toward the center of the city, the marketplace. The conspirators had stolen some Roman trumpets, which they used to sound an alarm for the Roman soldiers. As those soldiers streamed out of the garrison to answer the alarm, they were cut down quickly and quietly.

As morning broke, the citizens of Tarentum were awoken by town criers, who called on them to assemble in the marketplace. Cries of "Liberty" were mixed in, as well. When they arrived in the center of town, the citizens were astonished to find a large formation of Carthaginian soldiers and the legendary Hannibal, whom they had heard all about but never before seen. He raised his hand for quiet and began to talk to the crowd in their native language—Greek.

> You have nothing to fear. Go home, and each one of you write over his door "A Tarentine's House." Those words alone will be sufficient security; no door so marked will be violated. But the mark must not be set falsely on the door of any Roman house; [anyone] guilty of such treason will be put to death, for all Roman property in the normal prize of my soldiers.

The citizens returned to their homes, and Hannibal kept his promise. Only the wealthy Roman houses were looted, and only a handful of Carthaginian men had been killed. He had stolen a rich and prosperous Roman city.

ROMAN COUNTERATTACKS

The Romans decided they needed to take Capua back while Hannibal was in Tarentum. To do so, they assembled a very large army outside Capua and laid siege to the city. Word got to Hannibal that "his" Capua was under siege. He sent 2,000 of his Numidian soldiers there to buy some time. Even though the Roman army had tens of thousands of men, just the sight of the Numidians struck fear into the Romans, and they halted their siege. Soon after, Hannibal's army marched into Capua; at first, all the Roman armies could do was watch and be afraid. The citizens of Capua greeted Hannibal with tears of joy.

The Romans tried to counterattack, but there was so much confusion and fear of Hannibal that they soon broke it off and fled. The citizens of Capua looked at the deserted Roman camp and cheered. They felt nothing could harm them as long as Hannibal was near them. They were right.

Then a pattern developed. The Romans planned a counterattack on Tarentum when they knew Hannibal has marched to Capua. As Hannibal planned for a rescue at Tarentum, the Romans marched back to Capua and laid siege again. The Roman plan was to make any gains by Hannibal only temporary, and to focus on retaking whatever Hannibal had taken after he moved on. That way, citizens would know that Rome was not giving up and that they would be penalized for conspiring with Hannibal.

HANNIBAL AT THE GATES

Hannibal decided that, to protect both Capua and Tarentum, he needed to threaten the city of Rome itself. He marched his army to the very edge of the city's enormous walls. He rode with a group of his Numidian cavalry around the city walls, to let the

en afrique.

Ly fine le quatriefme liure
de ce prefent traittie l'Homme

A large part of Hannibal's success is credited to his ability to create alliances with tribes who were unfriendly toward his enemy. With the help of the Gallic tribes from France and Numidians from Africa, Hannibal managed to organize his diverse troops into a fearsome army.

Romans see him and fear him in person. For the first time, he was at their gates. Rome didn't dare send out troops to attack him, but the city also knew that thousands of their troops stood inside the wall, ready to protect the citizens against this deadliest of enemies.

At one point, Hannibal took a javelin from one his cavalrymen and threw it high over the towering outer wall at the Colline Gate. Hannibal knew the power of symbolism—that one javelin must have struck fear into every Roman who saw it, thinking that thousands more were to follow. They now saw the physical strength of this one man. Yet, that single javelin was the only weapon the Carthaginians ever used against the Romans inside their city walls. Hannibal threw it out of both defiance and frustration. He knew he would never attack Rome successfully without many more men. He must have known that his brother Hasdrubal would soon be bringing those men.

Hannibal's "attack" on Rome cost him Tarentum. Fabius took the chance to march on Tarentum and retook the city. When Hannibal arrived there after his Roman expedition, he could only look at the walls, which were filled with Roman soldiers staring down at him. Hannibal tried to trick Fabius into coming out of the city to fight him, but Fabius had too much discipline, or luck, to do so.

Rome was heartened by news that Tarentum had been taken back, and the citizens were relieved that Hannibal had not tried to storm their city. The senate authorized the recruitment of more troops to fight Hannibal and began to look for new leadership of its various armies.

HANNIBAL'S GREATEST FOE

The 17-year-old son of the Roman general Scipio who had saved his father during the battle at the Ticinus River 10 years earlier was now 27. He had grown up to be an extraordinary man. He was highly intelligent—educated by his father and tutors in Greek culture and in warfare—and articulate and confident when he spoke. He was strong and athletic, and he had a commanding presence. He was remarkably like a young Hannibal. He had seen Hannibal in action at several battles and had studied his tactics and strategies. He learned well.

He asked the Roman Senate to put him in charge of the army in Spain, where he had most recently served. Many older senators argued that he was too young to assume command. He did not honor all the Roman traditions of discipline and duty—he had been seen with many women and much wine, and even dressed in comfortable clothes. He did not seem like a conventional Roman general, who would emphasize strength in numbers and blunt warfare over surprise and innovative battle tactics. He believed in forming alliances and using diplomacy if possible, not just sheer military might. He simply was not like the traditional generals (who had lost every battle to Hannibal). There were, however, enough Roman senators who wanted a change that he was elected to command the Roman armies in Spain. It would prove to be one of the most far-reaching military appointments in ancient world history.

Scipio the Younger went back to Spain in 209 B.C. as a commander and did exactly what no traditional Roman general would have done—he attacked New Carthage. Traditional Roman strategy would have fought battles against the Carthaginian army in Spain instead of attacking a city that only had about 1,000 Carthaginian soldiers protecting the town of 20,000. First, Scipio found out everything he could about New Carthage. He asked questions of everyone, including fishermen who knew about the tides in the bay below New Carthage. He came up with a brilliant and innovative plan to do something no one expected—to carry out a simultaneous land and sea attack, with several elements of surprise. He would do what Hannibal would have done.

On the day of the attack, he placed his ships at the edge of the bay and fired missiles from catapults. He had his land-based troops use scaling ladders to climb the walls of the city. While the Carthaginian soldiers ran to defend those walls, Scipio had other men carry ladders across a marshy lagoon at lowest tide and climb a wall no one was defending. His soldiers streamed into the city and, in a matter of two hours, captured it.

Scipio then did something else extraordinary, something that Hannibal would not have done: He gave all the citizens of New Carthage the freedom to go. He declared the wealth of the city to be the property of his soldiers and the Roman people, but he did not want to enslave the citizens. He also released all of the hostages the Carthaginians had taken over the years to keep the Iberian tribes in check. When a beautiful Spanish woman hostage was brought to him as a gift from his officers,

Another Cleopatra

Leaders of any kind often have very strong and complicated personal relationships that sometimes change their public power. They are driven people, and they attract similarly driven people. The world has come to know the story of Cleopatra and Antony: Cleopatra was the extraordinarily beautiful and intelligent queen of Egypt, and Mark Antony was a conquering hero and leader of Rome who fell hopelessly in love with her. He betrayed his duties and country for her. Antony committed suicide when he thought Cleopatra was dead, and she killed herself when she heard of her lover's death—and when she thought she would be captured and marched through Rome as a villain. Personal and political lives are so intertwined that it is hard to see where one ends and the other begins.

Historians note that there was a second Cleopatra in the ancient world. Her name was Sophonisba, and she was a young and beautiful Numidian princess who was married to Syphax, the king of Massaeylia (now Algeria) in North Africa. Syphax was part of the Carthaginian force defeated by Scipio in North Africa, and Sophonisba was about to be taken prisoner and dragged away in shame by the Romans. She arranged to meet with the young Numidian cavalry leader Masinissa to plead for her husband's life (and for her own as well). Masinissa was one of Scipio's great cavalry commanders, and so was very influential. When Masinissa met Sophonisba, he fell in love at first sight. She had legendary beauty and a personal power he could not resist. They

Scipio discovered that she was engaged to a tribal nobleman already. He summoned the man and presented the woman to him. In gratitude, the tribal warrior was from that day forward a valuable ally of Scipio. The young commander knew how to use diplomacy as well as force.

seduced each other immediately and became so inseparable, so fast, that they were soon secretly married—even though she was already married to Syphax.

Scipio knew that he had a real problem on his hands. Sophonisba was very capable of turning Masinissa away from the Romans and perhaps even making him fight for the remaining Carthaginian army. Scipio called Masinissa to his tent and told him how important their friendship was to him and to Rome. The Roman historian Livy quotes Scipio as saying: "You committed yourself and all your hope to my protection. But of all those virtues which made me seem worthy of your regard, there is none of which I am so proud as temperance and control of my passions." Scipio was masterful at making Masinissa feel ashamed and regretful of his loss of control for a woman he just met. Masinissa left the tent in tears, the fever of his passion broken. He then did something dramatic and painful: He sent Sophonisba a cup that contained poison, and he told her she must drink it because he could not be her husband and she could not fall into the hands of the Romans. She wrote him a message back:

> I accept this nuptial present; nor is it an unwelcome one, if my husband can render me no better service. Tell him, however, that I should have died with greater satisfaction had I not married so near to my death.

She signed the letter, drank the poison, and died, yet another victim of the long war.

THE HEAD OF HASDRUBAL

Historians have speculated about why Scipio decided to take New Carthage when a Carthaginian army in Spain could retake the city soon after. The main Carthaginian army in Spain was led by Hannibal's brother Hasdrubal. Whether Scipio knew it or not, Hasdrubal was soon headed to Italy by almost the same route his brother had taken 11 years earlier. Without additional men, Hannibal was only able to engage in holding actions in southern Italy; Hasdrubal was going to bring a second Carthaginian army to his brother's aid. The armies of the sons of Hamilcar would meet and probably attack Rome once and for all.

Hasdrubal must have found some of the roads that Hannibal's men built through the Alps. He was not attacked by the same tribes that had harassed his brother years earlier. The costs of the earlier battles with Hannibal would have been fresh in the minds of the Volcae, the Allobroges, and the mountain people. He did not have to pass through the highest part of the mountains because he was not counting on surprising anyone. The Romans must have known that Hannibal needed reinforcements.

In the early spring of 207 B.C., Hasdrubal and his army of men and elephants crossed over the Alps and into the Po River Valley in northern Italy. Hasdrubal wrote his brother a long letter, which spelled out exactly where and when they should meet to combine their two armies. He gave the letter to a group of his six best horsemen and told them to take the letter to Hannibal at all costs, and to avoid capture by the Romans. The six rode out—traveling only at night—toward Hannibal's camp in Apulia. They arrived there quickly and safely, but, as fate would have it, Hannibal had just moved his army away from Apulia. Somehow, the messengers were then captured by a few Roman soldiers on patrol near Tarentum. The messengers could not (or did not) destroy the letter fast enough. Historians to this day are amazed that Hasdrubal did not use a code of some sort—such codes existed, and for a document of this importance to be written in Punic for all to read is a mystery. As a result, Hannibal never received the letter. The Roman Senate did.

The Romans now had an enormous advantage: They knew their enemy's plan. They sent two armies to the area where Hasdrubal was to meet Hannibal, and they disguised the size of their force by hiding several men in every small tent. Hasdrubal's scouts dramatically misjudged the size of the Roman force. The Romans met the Carthaginians at the Metaurus River in Umbria. Hasdrubal was not his brother, and he did not create a battle plan that would win the battle before it even began. The sheer numbers of the Roman soldiers won the day, especially after Hasdrubal's elephants panicked and stampeded over many of their own men.

When Hasdrubal saw that he was going to lose the battle, he rode his horse directly into the middle of a Roman line and died fighting. Without their leader, his men soon gave up and fled. Ten thousand Carthaginians were killed or captured that day. As Hannibal waited for word from his brother, he received another kind of message. The severed head of Hasdrubal was thrown into his camp by Roman cavalrymen.

SCIPIO BECOMES HANNIBAL

Rome was overjoyed at the news that Hasdrubal had been defeated, and Hannibal was on his own. The entire political climate began to change. The Roman Senate was soon ready for the bolder strategies of Scipio, who proposed that his army attack Carthage in North Africa. It was a daring plan. Hannibal would be forced to leave Italy and defend Carthage, and he would know that Scipio could win—he had already taken New Carthage in Spain. The old guard in the Roman Senate disagreed, saying that Scipio was needed to protect Rome from Hannibal. Once again, Scipio prevailed because of a series of speeches he made in the senate. He was forceful and articulate, and only the small-minded and jealous older men tried to undermine him.

In the spring of 204 B.C., Scipio sailed from Italy with 40 warships, 400 transport ships, and 20,000 men, and landed in North Africa near the Carthaginian town of Utica. He had studied Hannibal's tactics so well that he knew he needed something Hannibal had always possessed—a Numidian cavalry. He recruited a brilliant young Numidian prince, Masinissa, whom he had known in Spain. He studied the tactics Hannibal had used at Trebbia, especially hiding the Numidian cavalry and using them to swing the battle at a key moment. He knew he wanted to use surprise, as Hannibal always had. He added his own innovation first used at New Carthage—a combined land and sea force. He then used a tactic he had never used before. His spies noticed that the Carthaginian armies always placed their huts close together, and that the huts were made of reed or straw. He knew they would burn quickly and completely. He did not need to drop firebombs, as later military leaders would; the huts themselves would become bombs.

The Carthaginian army in North Africa wanted to draw Scipio into a battle on the open plains. Scipio was too smart for that, since he had far fewer men than the Carthaginians. Instead, he faked an advance on the enemy army near Utica and then waited until night to send in raiders to set fire to the Carthaginian huts. The roaring fires spread so rapidly that the Carthaginian soldiers were trapped, and thousands died from the flames. Others were killed as they ran from the fires, past Scipio's waiting legions. The fires spread so high that all of Utica could see them. When it was over, approximately 40,000 Carthaginian soldiers were dead in a smoldering black field.

In a few other small battles, Scipio and his forces could not be beat by the depleted Carthaginian army, just as Hannibal could not be beat in Italy. Scipio used both his army and his

The Romans sent a very direct message to Hannibal after defeating and killing his brother Hasdrubal. They threw Hasdrubal's head into the Carthaginian general's camp, taunting him with their victory.

navy to bring Carthage down. Carthage asked for a truce and agreed to terms of peace: All Carthaginian troops would be brought home from Italy, and Carthage would give up all but 20 of its ships. Thus, Hannibal was called home.

7

War of
the Worlds

IT WAS 202 B.C., AND HANNIBAL HAD BEEN AWAY FROM CARTHAGE SINCE he was 9 years old, and away from New Carthage since he was 28. He was now 45. He had kept his oath to his father and fought Rome wherever he could. But he had been changed by Italy, just as he had changed it. He loved Apulia and its people.

Roman commanders watched as Hannibal and his men loaded into a ship bound for North Africa. They probably had orders to try to delay his return but could only look on in relief to finally see their enemy leaving. As he sailed away from the Italian coast for the last time, Hannibal must have been overwhelmed with both memories and expectations. He had lost his brother Hasdrubal not long before, and he must have known what was ahead. He was on a collision course with Scipio and the biggest battle of his life.

The Greatest Military Leader in the Ancient World

Historians can argue endlessly about who was the greatest military leader in the ancient world. Roman historian Acilius records that Scipio and Hannibal actually discussed the subject. Hannibal told Scipio that Alexander the Great was the greatest leader, "because with a small force he defeated armies whose numbers were beyond reckoning, and because he overran the remotest regions." Hannibal felt that Pyrrhus was the second greatest leader, partly because he "possessed the art of conciliating mankind." Hannibal felt he was the third greatest leader.

Scipio then asked Hannibal, "What would you have said if you had conquered me?" Hannibal replied, "Then I would have placed Hannibal not only before Alexander and Pyrrhus, but before all other commanders." With that answer, Hannibal finally managed to flatter Scipio (though in a backhanded sort of way), which pleased the Roman leader. Many historians think Hannibal was the most unselfish of the ancient leaders, always more concerned for his culture than for himself or his family. Scipio, Alexander, and Pyrrhus were all geniuses as well, but they were more willing to accept individual glory and fame.

Many historians now argue that the greatest leader of the ancient world may have been Alexander the Great's father, Philip II of Macedon. It was Philip who created the model for an integrated cavalry and infantry, and expanded the Macedonian Empire through a combination of warfare and diplomacy. He seemed to know when and who to fight, and when not to fight, to bring more wealth and security to his people. His son only had to watch and learn.

BREAKING THE TRUCE

Hannibal landed in his homeland at Leptis, in the Gulf of Hammamet. He soon heard that his fellow Carthaginians had broken the truce with Scipio: Some leaders had seized 200 transport ships that were bringing supplies to Scipio. This was a clear violation of a negotiated peace.

Many Carthaginians felt that—because Hannibal was back in North Africa—he would protect them, and that they did not have to honor the truce terms laid down by the Romans. The Carthaginian government told Hannibal to attack Scipio. Hannibal sent them a note in return that said he would not be told what to do.

Hannibal decided to increase his troop strength. He asked a Numidian chief, Tychaeus, to send his best cavalrymen. He recalled Carthaginian soldiers from Spain and other areas. He asked other enemies of Rome to send troops, and Philip of Macedon sent approximately 4,000 men. With 24,000 men returning from Italy and still with him, Hannibal soon had an imposing army of 50,000 troops, many of whom were experienced in combat.

Scipio was angered by the breaking of the truce and knew that Hannibal was building his army. Scipio decided to march his men away from Carthage and make Hannibal come to him. He also needed to wait for the return of Masinissa, who had assumed that the truce would hold. Masinissa had traveled to Rome to be treated as a hero and given the title of king. Scipio and Masinissa arranged to meet up near the town of Zama, about five days' journey west of Carthage.

THE GREAT MEETING

Hannibal sent scouts to determine where Scipio was and to assess his troop strength. Hannibal was not surprised when some of the scouts returned and said that three scouts had been captured by Scipio when they ventured too close to the Roman

Impressed by Scipio's unusual generosity in taking care of his scouts instead of killing them, Hannibal met with the Roman general in an attempt to avoid battle and talk of peace.

camp near Zama. Scouts were often in danger, and Hannibal assumed they would be tortured and killed. So, he was amazed when he saw the three captured scouts ride into camp, unharmed and confused. Scipio had taken the scouts on a tour of his army, making sure he showed them everything they wished to see. He fed them and sent them back to Hannibal.

Hannibal was so impressed by the most unusual tactic that he did something very few commanders ever do: He asked for a meeting. Scipio agreed. At a neutral site near the modern Tunisian-Algerian border, two opposing groups of men faced each other, and three rode forward to meet. One was Hannibal, one was Scipio, and the third an interpreter. The Greek historian Polybius says that the two enemies stared at each other face to face for some time, without speaking. Hannibal broke the silence.

Hannibal and Our World

Hannibal still exerts an enormous influence on our modern world. His crossing of the Alps remains one of the most storied feats in world history. Major motion pictures about Hannibal began as early as the movie industry itself began, from 1914's silent movie *Cabiria* to 1939's *The Defeat of Hannibal* to 1960's *Annibale* (starring Victor Mature). In 2006, a movie made for television called *Hannibal: Rome's Worst Nightmare* played to world audiences. The National Geographic Channel showed *Hannibal vs. Rome* in 2005. Three major documentaries have been made in the past decade. Three novels about Hannibal appeared in 2005–2006, including David Anthony Durham's *Pride of Carthage.*

Hannibal is still studied at military academies all over the world, along with Alexander the Great, Julius Caesar, Robert E. Lee, Erwin Rommel, Napoleon Bonaparte, and Frederick the Great. U.S. general Norman Schwarzkopf, the commander of the Coalition Forces in the First Gulf War, said that the same principles of war he used in 1991 applied in Hannibal's day. An article in the *Encyclopedia Britannica* summarizes Hannibal's lasting military influence:

> The man who for fifteen years could hold his ground in a hostile country against several powerful armies and a succession of able generals must have been a commander and tactician of supreme capacity. . . . We never hear of a mutiny in his army, composed though it was of Africans, Iberians, and Gauls. All we know of him comes from hostile sources. The Romans feared and hated him so much they could not do him justice. . . . For steadfastness of purpose, for organizing capacity, and a mastery of military science he has perhaps never had an equal.

Would that neither the Romans had never coveted any pos-
sessions outside Italy; nor the Carthaginians any outside
Africa, for both these were very fine empires, and empires
of which it might be said that Nature herself had fixed their
limits. But now . . . what remains but to consider by what
means we can avert the anger of the gods? I myself am ready
to do so as I learnt by experience how fickle Fortune is. . . .
What man of sense, I ask, would rush into such danger as
that which confronts you now? If you conquer you will add
but little to the fame of your country and your own, but if
you suffer defeat you will utterly deface the memory of all
that was grand and glorious in your past.

Hannibal tried to convince Scipio to avoid further war, since he
had much to lose and little to gain.

Scipio was the younger man, and the more confident that
day—Masinissa had joined him with 10,000 more men. Scipio
spoke. He reminded Hannibal that the Carthaginians broke the
truce agreement and did not live up to its conditions.

What remains to be done? Put yourself in my place and tell
me. Shall we withdraw the most onerous conditions imposed
[by the truce]? That would be to reward your countrymen
for their treachery. . . . Of what further use then is this inter-
view? Either put yourselves and your country at our mercy
or fight and conquer us.

There was no reconciliation. The two commanders rode away
from each other, and all knew that the next day would bring
war. The next battle would be a war unto itself and would
decide the future of both Rome and Carthage.

MASSACRE AT ZAMA

For the first time in his life, Hannibal did not have the superior battle plan when his army marched onto the battlefield

During the Battle of Zama, Scipio mimicked the tried-and-true methods Hannibal used in his most famous battles, yet also employed new tactics that confused and damaged the Carthaginian forces.

at dawn. Scipio had learned from his master, and he had drawn up a plan that drew on Hannibal's success at Cannae. First, Scipio arranged his legions in blocks, with large lanes in between them, to let the 80 Carthaginian elephants roam free without doing as much damage to the Romans as they had in past battles. Next, Scipio told his cavalry to be ready to retreat on a signal and then regroup and hit the Carthaginians from another angle.

Hannibal used his tactics from Cannae. He led with his elephants (80 was the most he had ever used in a battle) and arranged his soldiers in three groups, in order of experience. His most experienced were at the rear, ready to fight when the Romans became exhausted from fighting the less experienced troops. As always, the ranks were to fall back and not get in one another's way. No inexperienced fighters were allowed to fight side by side with experienced ones. Hannibal would rely on his ability to surround the Romans. He had the strength of numbers, probably about 55,000 men to oppose Scipio's 36,000.

The battle began with Hannibal's elephants charging. As the beasts came near the front lines of the Romans, they heard a blast of hundreds of war trumpets and a tremendous shout. Many of the elephants panicked and turned on their own men. Some made it to the Roman lines, but several were funneled down the open lanes between the legions.

The Roman legions fought the first two Carthaginian lines to a draw, with many losses on each side. When the Romans had fought their way to the third group—the "Old Guard" veterans who had been with Hannibal in Italy—Scipio did something extraordinary: He sounded a retreat. His troops all spoke one language, unlike Hannibal's, so they could communicate with one another on the battlefield better than the Carthaginians could. Scipio then re-formed his troops into a long line, a tactic almost never used in battle in the ancient world. In doing so, he spread out the opposition, but he took the risk of having his line broken at any point and the pieces devoured by Hannibal's experienced men.

At a crucial point, Masinissa and his Numidian cavalry reentered the battle, but this time from the side and the rear. Hannibal had won at Cannae by surrounding his enemy. Scipio won at Zama the same way. The experienced Carthaginian soldiers fought well and bravely, but eventually they were surrounded by the cavalry and the extended line of Roman troops and cut down one by one. They were massacred. Before long, 20,000 of them lay dead. The Battle of Zama was over, and so was the Second Punic War. It had lasted 17 years, and, as a result, the balance of power in the ancient world had changed dramatically and for generations to come. In the coming centuries, students and scholars would not learn Carthaginian—they would learn Latin.

8

Fighting
to the End

HANNIBAL ESCAPED FROM THE BATTLEFIELD AT ZAMA AFTER HE HAD DONE everything he could. It was the first time he ever left a battlefield in defeat. He knew that he could be a valuable leader in Carthage even after his years as a commander were over. He knew that he could help negotiate terms of surrender with Scipio and Rome, and he hoped he could help rebuild Carthage. He was valuable in restraining the remaining war parties in his own country, mostly old men who could not believe they had lost to Rome and who still wanted to wage a war to the last soldier. One Carthaginian senator gave a long speech about how Carthage must remain strong, stay the course, and continue to try to defeat Rome. Hannibal walked up to the podium, where the senator was urging that more young Carthaginian lives be spent, and physically pulled the senator down. His actions spoke louder than words.

Rome dictated the peace terms, which were that Carthage destroy its navy and surrender all its war elephants. Carthage was to no longer expand beyond a specific area in North Africa and was to pay Rome a large sum of money, made in 50 annual installments. Five hundred Carthaginian warships were then

The Roman Triumph

Scipio was one of the first to receive a Roman triumph—a civil ceremony and religious rite to honor the military commander of a successful and large foreign war. To be eligible for a triumph, the commander must have killed at least 5,000 enemy soldiers and brought his army home, showing that the war was over.

The ceremony was a spectacular parade. Wagons of gold and other valuables captured in the war came first, followed by musicians and dancers with large drawings that showed key scenes from the war. Then came the victorious general, his face and arms painted red. He rode on a four-wheeled cart pulled by two white horses. A slave held a laurel crown over his head (the crown must not touch the head). The slave had to repeatedly say "Memento mori" ("Remember thou art mortal").

The parade usually started outside the Servian Walls of the city, on the western bank of the Tiber River. The triumphant general then went through Via Triumphalis and marched into the Roman Forum. Centuries later, Italian dictator Benito Mussolini would revive the tradition so that he too could march in triumph. (No one knows if he had a slave repeat the words "Memento mori.") Some time after his triumph, Mussolini was deposed and later found dead hanging from a meat hook in a plaza in Milan. He was indeed mortal.

towed out to sea and set afire. An empire had ended, and a new one was built in Rome.

Scipio returned to Rome and was given a triumph, a parade in which he rode through the streets in front of his troops. He was named Scipio Africanus, and so became the first of many Roman generals named after the country they conquered. He could have been named consul for life, but he declined. Later Roman leaders, called *ceasars*, would not decline the same offer.

HANNIBAL THE REFORMER

From 202 B.C. to 195 B.C., Hannibal served his country in a different way: He tried to heal the wounds of war. He and Scipio respected each other, and both worked to make sure the peace they had signed stayed in effect. Many in Rome wanted Hannibal's head to be delivered to Rome, but Scipio managed to keep the most warlike Romans in check, at least for a few years. The Roman senator Cato allegedly ended every speech, no matter the subject, with "Carthage must be destroyed."

In 200 B.C., Hannibal was elected chief magistrate of Carthage, and he set about trying to reform the government. He knew that certain officials were corrupt and were stealing public funds. Hannibal would not stand for corruption, or even favoritism. He had fought too long and too hard for his country to see it run by a few officials trying to get rich and reward their friends. He introduced many reforms to help improve life in Carthage, and eventually businesses began to grow again. Yet, he made several powerful enemies when he cleaned up corruption. First, these enemies tried to have judges find a crime of which Hannibal might be found guilty. Then they told Rome that Hannibal was plotting against them. Scipio had to make a speech to the Roman Senate to assure them that Hannibal had done no wrong and that his enemies in Carthage were plotting against him.

Returning to Rome with 123,000 pounds of silver taken in battle, Scipio presented his bounty to the senate and was renamed Scipio Africanus. He retired from battle after defeating Hannibal and pursued a political career.

Hannibal survived for four years as a magistrate. He brought many reforms to Carthage and guided the city during a very difficult time after the defeat by Rome. It was no longer a powerful empire, but people's lives were improving and some businesses were successful.

BECOMING A MERCENARY

The Roman leader Cato was able to stir up enough fear of Hannibal rising again that, in 195 B.C., a large Roman delegation was sent to Carthage to open an inquiry into Hannibal's actions. Scipio was no longer influential enough to stop the men in Rome who were still scared of Hannibal. Hannibal realized that his enemies in Carthage were powerful enough to sell him out, and he believed he had no choice but to leave or be captured by the Romans. He sailed for Tyre with his family, worried more about the fate of his country than about what was going to happen to him and his loved ones.

He first went to Antiochus III, king of Seleucia in Asia Minor and a known enemy of Rome. Antiochus was a ruler of an empire in what is now Syria, and he wanted to expand westward into Greece. The Romans were also expanding in that direction, and Antiochus put Hannibal in charge of his navy in an effort to stop Rome. The Romans came in search of Hannibal, and, when Antiochus was defeated in the Battle of Magnesia in 190 B.C., Hannibal knew he had to flee again.

This time, he and his family went to the island of Crete. Hannibal had been well paid by Antiochus, and he settled into a villa in Crete. He spent a good deal of time in his garden, where several bronze statues secretly contained his wealth in the form of many gold coins. When the Cretans realized who their new guest was, they required him to place some of these riches in narrow-necked jars in the Temple of Diana as an offering. Hannibal secretly filled the jars with lead and placed a few gold coins on top, and the authorities never knew the difference. The jars were sealed and closely guarded by the Cretans. Little did they know they were guarding more lead than gold.

Ancient Poisons

No one knows which poison Hannibal took to end his life. He had several to choose from. The Greeks called aconite (also known as wolfsbane) the "Queen of Poisons," and in ancient times, it was the deadliest poison known. Extracted from the plant monkshood, it was also used to poison the tips of arrows and javelins. Greek legend said it was made from the saliva of Cerberus, the three-headed dog that guarded the underworld.

Egyptian papyrus scrolls dated to near the time of Hannibal record the process of extracting and concentrating a juice from peach pits. We now know this as prussic acid, more commonly called cyanide. Roman emperor Nero later became famous for using the poison at the dinner table to wipe out several political rivals and family members. Adolf Hitler ended his life using cyanide.

Perhaps the most likely poison Hannibal used was hemlock. It was sanctioned for use in situations where suicide was a noble act, and Hannibal must have felt that his death qualified as noble. In 399 B.C., Socrates famously drank a cup of hemlock after being found guilty of corrupting youth. In small doses, hemlock is a medicine, and the ancient world used it for various ailments. In large doses, it is deadly. Death occurs within two hours, after all sensation is lost and a kind of paralysis sets in. For many years, in various ancient cultures, hemlock was used to administer the death penalty.

Hannibal executed himself so Rome could not. If he had been captured and brought to Rome, crucifixion would have been his fate. Crucifixion was a combination of public torture and slow execution of enemies of the state. Hannibal would never have let Rome exert that final power over him.

Prusias, ruler of a country named Bithynia in Asia Minor (near the Black Sea), then asked Hannibal to help him fight a war against Rome. Hannibal loaded his household goods and several bronze statues from his garden, and moved his family to Bithynia, a beautiful region with lakes, trees, and wonderful mountain views. The Cretans continued to closely guard the jars in the temple of Diana; they let Hannibal leave with his garden statues without even looking into them.

THE DYING DAYS

Prusias fought the Roman armies from 187 B.C. to 183 B.C. and then surrendered. As part of the terms for surrender, he was required to give Hannibal to the Romans so they could take him back to Rome as a prisoner. When Hannibal saw that Roman guards had surrounded his villa, he knew there was no escape. He would not be taken prisoner and marched though the streets of Rome in a mock triumph.

Instead, Hannibal swallowed a dose of poison. His last words before death were, "Let us now put an end to the life that has caused the Romans so much anxiety." When news of his death reached Rome, the city celebrated. Much of Carthage mourned. Hannibal was 64 years old.

Thirty-seven years after the death of Hannibal, Carthage was wiped from the face of the earth during the Third Punic War, which lasted from 149 B.C. to 146 B.C. The city was under siege for three years and was burned to the ground by fires that lasted 17 days. Its massive city walls were completely destroyed. Every trace of civilization was buried. The jewel of the Mediterranean was pulverized and turned into small particles of dust. Legend has it that the Romans even scattered salt all around the city ruins so nothing would ever grow there again. Historians say that Rome then tried to destroy the very idea of Carthage. One hundred years later, however, Julius Caesar sent Roman

Rather than suffer the indignity of being paraded throughout Rome, Hannibal spared himself this fate by drinking a cup of poison. Hannibal's bold military strategy and brilliant leadership has been well documented in books, movies, and even video games.

troops to the site to start a new colony in the strategic spot. Life began again.

Rome did not kill the idea of Carthage, and today we still study Hannibal and his legacy. Romans built statues in the streets of Rome to advertise their defeat of such a worthy adversary. He is a towering figure in world history, a true leader who was ruthless, innovative, successful, and self-sacrificing. He emboldened his followers. He frightened his enemies; for centuries following the death of Hannibal, Roman mothers could be heard saying to their children, when they wanted them to listen and behave, "Hannibal ad portas!" ("Hannibal is at the gates"). No greater horror could have been imagined. No greater force swept through the ancient world.

CHRONOLOGY

◆ ◆ ◆

(All dates are B.C.)

814–800	Carthage is founded.
753	Rome is founded.
509	Romans overthrow king-tyrant and begin a republic.
264	First Punic War begins between Rome and Carthage, essentially a naval war for island of Sicily.
246	Hannibal Barca born in Carthage, son of warrior Hamilcar Barca.
241	Romans win Battle of Aegates, and Carthage is forced to negotiate terms of peace; First Punic War ends.
238	Hamilcar Barca, Hannibal's father, is sent to Iberia to expand Carthage's empire.
237	Hannibal joins his father in Iberia.
229	Hannibal's father is killed.
221	Hannibal becomes commander of the Carthaginian army in Iberia (now Spain).
218	Rome declares war on Carthage, and Second Punic War begins. Hannibal leaves Iberia for Italy, crossing the Alps. His army enters Italy and wins a battle at Trebbia.

217	Hannibal defeats a Roman army at Lake Trasimene.
216	Hannibal destroys Roman armies at Cannae.
214	Hannibal visits the Lake of the Dead.
213	Hannibal captures key city of Tarentum in southern Italy.
211	Hannibal marches to the gates of Rome.
209	Hannibal loses Tarentum; Scipio the Younger attacks New Carthage in Iberia.
207	Hannibal's brother Hasdrubal is killed at battle of Metaurus trying to bring an army to reinforce Hannibal's; Scipio the Younger increases Roman forces in Iberia.
204	Romans, led by Scipio, land in North Africa.
203–202	Hannibal is recalled from Italy to defend Carthage.
202	Scipio defeats Hannibal at the Battle of Zama in North Africa; Carthage accepts peace terms, and the Second Punic War is ended.
200	As chief magistrate of Carthage, Hannibal reforms the city government.
195	Hannibal is forced to leave Carthage; he joins forces with Roman enemy Antiochus III.
190	Antiochus loses Battle of Magnesia, and Hannibal leaves for Crete.
187	Hannibal joins King Prusias in Bithynia (Asia Minor) to help fight Romans there.
183	Hannibal is surrounded by Roman soldiers at his villa in Bithynia, takes poison, and dies.
149	Third Punic War begins; Romans lay siege to Carthage.
146	Romans destroy every trace of Carthage, and Third Punic War ends.

BIBLIOGRAPHY

◆ ◆ ◆

Bradford, Alfred S. *With Arrow, Sword, and Spear.* New York: Praeger Publishing, 2001.

Church, Alfred J. "Helmet and Spear," *The Baldwin Project,* 2006. Available online. http://www.mainlesson.com.

Cottrell, Leonard. *Hannibal: Enemy of Rome.* New York: Da Capo Press, 1961.

Daly, Gregory. *Cannae: The Experience of Battle in the Second Punic War.* London: Routledge, 2002.

Dodge, Theodore A. *Hannibal: A History of the Art of War Among the Carthaginians and Romans Down to the Battle of Pydna, 168 B.C.* New York: Da Capo Press, 1995.

Fournie, Daniel. "Second Punic War: Hannibal's War in Italy," *Military History,* March/April 2005. Available online. http://TheHistoryNet.com.

Gabriel, Richard A. *The Great Armies of Antiquity.* New York: Praeger Publishing, 2002.

Holland, Tom. "Elephant Man," *Daily Mail,* May 6, 2006. Available online. http://www.highbeam.com.

Hoyos, Dexter. *Hannibal's Dynasty: Power and Politics in the Western Mediterranean, 247–183 B.C.* London: Routledge, 2003.

Prevas, John. *Hannibal Crosses the Alps.* New York: Da Capo Press, 1998.

FURTHER READING

◆ ◆ ◆

Daly, Gregory. *Cannae: The Experience of Battle in the Second Punic War.* London: Routledge, 2002.

Dodge, Theodore A. *Hannibal: A History of the Art of War Among the Carthaginians and Romans Down to the Battle of Pydna, 168 B.C.* New York: Da Capo Press, 1995.

Gabriel, Richard A. *The Great Armies of Antiquity.* New York: Praeger Publishing, 2002.

Keegan, John. *A History of Warfare.* New York: Vintage, 1993.

Prevas, John. *Hannibal Crosses the Alps.* New York: Da Capo Press, 1998.

WEB SITES

Ancient Historians
www.livius.org

Ancient History Sourcebooks
www.fordham.edu/halsall/ancient/polybius-hannibal.html

Classics History
www.mainlesson.com

Military History
www.TheHistoryNet.com

PHOTO CREDITS

◆ ◆ ◆

INDEX

A

aconite, 107
Aeneas, 27
African horsemen. *See* Numidians
Alexander the Great, 58, 94
Allobroge tribe, 52–53
Alpes du Dauphiné, 50
Alps, as barrier, 16, 18
Alps crossing
    battle with mountain people, 55–58
    beginning the climb, 50–51
    descending into Italy, 59–60, 62
    fighting the Allobroges, 52–53
Antiochus III, 106
Antony, Mark, 86
Apulia, 72, 79, 93
archeological evidence, 23
Ares, 47
army, Hannibal's
    Alps crossing. *See* Alps crossing
    assembly of, 23–24
    battles of. *See* battles
    elephants in, 19, 56, 62, 69, 99–100
    enters Italy, 59–60, 62
    leadership of, 20–21
    leaves Italy, 93–94
    Pyrenees crossing, 41–43
    Rhône River crossing, 44–48
    size of, 23–24
    soldier composition of, 18–19
    speeches to, 21–23, 50–51
army, Roman, 30, 61
Athens, navy of, 31

B

Baal, 46
Barca family, 14, 21, 36, 37
battle strategies. *See* military tactics
battles. *See also* naval battles
    with Allobroge, 52–53
    Cannae, 70–74
    Lake Trasimene, 69–70
    with mountain people, 55–58
    Ticinus River, 62–64
    Trebbia, 66–69
    Zama, 98–101
Bithynia, 108
books about Hannibal, 97
brothers, 37, 41, 42, 88–89

C

Cannae, battle of, 70–74
Capua, 77, 82
Carthage
    corruption in, 104
    destruction of, 108
    end of empire, 102–104
    founding of, 26
    gods of, 46–47
    legacy of, 110
    navy of, 31, 32
    original name of, 26
    rise of, 27–29

Scipio's defeat of, 89–92
truces with Rome, 92, 103–104
wars against Rome. *See* Punic
  wars
Cato, 104, 106
cavalry, 58. *See also* Numidians
Celtiberians, 37–38
Celtic tribes, 42, 45–48
chief magistrate of Carthage,
  Hannibal as, 104, 106
citizenship, Roman, 30
Claudius Pulcher, 34
Cleopatra, 86
coins, as historical source, 22
Col de Perthus, 42
commander in Spain, 39
corvus, 32
Crete, 106–108
crucifixion, 107
cyanide, 107

D

death of Hannibal, 108
Dido. *See* Elissa
Didobal, 37
Diesel, Vin, 16–17
Diodorus, 55

E

eagle legend, 36–37
education of Hannibal, 36, 38
elephants, 19, 56, 62, 69, 99–100
Elissa, 26–27
equipment of Roman soldiers, 61
Eshmun, 46

F

Fabius Maximus, Quintus, 70, 75–76,
  77, 84
family, 37, 38–39. *See also* Barca
  family
father. *See* Hamilcar Barca
father of military strategy, 16
fighting ships, 31, 32
films about Hannibal, 97
First Punic War, 30–35
Flaminius, 69–70
forensic archeology, 23

G

Gaul, passage through, 43–44
Gauls, 17–18, 42, 44
Gladiator, 16
gods, Carthaginian, 46–47
Greek military strategy, 58

H

Hamilcar Barca, 14, 18, 34–36, 38
Hanno, 37, 42
harbors of Carthage, 27–28
Hasdrupal (brother), 37, 88–89
Hasdrupal (brother-in law), 14, 36,
  39
hemlock, 107
historical sources, 22–23
Hittites, 31
Homer, 78
horsemen. *See* cavalry; Numidians
human sacrifice, 36, 46, 47, 74

I

Iberian campaign, 35–36, 37–38, 39
Imilce, 18, 38
infantry, 58, 61
Italy, political structure of, 17

K

Kardt-Hadash, 26–27

L

Lake Avernus, 78
Lake Trasimene, battle at, 69–70
landslide in Alps, 60
leadership of Hannibal, 20–21,
  38, 39
legacy of Hannibal, 16, 71, 97, 110
legions, Roman, 61
love affair, 79

M

Mago, 37
maniples, 61
marriage, 38–39
Masinissa, 86–87, 90, 95, 98, 100

mercenaries
    Hannibal as, 106–108
    in Hannibal's army, 18–19
    mutiny threatened by, 42–43
Mercenary War, 35
military leaders of ancient world, 94
military tactics
    against Allobroges in Alps, 52–53
    at Cannae, 71, 72–73
    of Greeks, 58
    Hannibal's influence on, 16,
        71, 97
    at Lake Trasimene, 69–70
    of Scipio the Younger, 85–87, 90,
        98–99
    at Ticinus River, 63–64
    at Trebbia, 66–68
    against Volcae at Rhône
        crossing, 45–48
    at Zama, 98–100
military training of Hannibal, 36,
    37, 39
monuments, as historical source, 23
mother, 37
mountain people, 55–58
mountain ranges, 16
movies about Hannibal, 97
Mussolini, Benito, 103
mutiny threatened by mercenaries,
    42–43

N

Naples, siege of, 77
naval battles, 31, 32–34
navy of Carthage, 31, 32
Nebuchadnezzar, 27
necropolis, 47
New Carthage
    army assembles in, 23–24
    founding of, 14
    Hannibal's speech in, 21–23
    location of, 13
    Scipio's conquest of, 85–86
nomad, 19
North Africa, racial diversity of, 16–17
novels about Hannibal, 97
Numidians
    in Hannibal's battle tactics,
        63–64, 67, 72–73, 82

military effectiveness of, 19
Scipio's use of, 90, 100

O

oath to fight Rome, 14, 36
Odysseus, 78
Odyssey (Homer), 78

P

Paullus, Lucius Aemilius, 70–71, 72
peace terms, 103–104
Philip II of Macedon, 58, 94
Phoenicians, 25–26
pincer movement, 71
Pliny the Elder, 55
Po Valley, 62–64
poisons, 107
Polybius, 22
Prusias, 108
prussic acid, 107
psychological motivation for war, 30
Punic wars
    First Punic War, 30–35
    historical sources on, 22–23
    Second Punic War, 39–40,
        100–101
    Third Punic War, 108
Pyrenees, 16, 41–43
Pyrrhus, 94

Q

quinqueremes, 32

R

racial diversity of North Africa, 16–17
reformer of Carthaginian
    government, 104, 106
religion, 46–47, 78
Rhône River, 44–48
Roman army encounters Hannibal's
    army, 48, 50
Roman legions, 61
Roman triumph ceremony, 103, 104
Rome
    after defeat at Cannae, 74
    after defeat at Lake Trasimene,
        70

domination of Italy by, 17
Hannibal at the gates of, 82–84
Hannibal proclaims war on, 21
plan for war on, 15, 16–18
rise of, 29–30
wars against Carthage. *See*
Punic wars

S

Saguntum, 39–40
Schwarzkopf, Norman, 71, 97
Scipio Africanus. *See* Scipio the
Younger
Scipio, Cornelius, 48, 50, 62–64
Scipio the Younger
appointed commander in Spain,
84–85
at battle of Zama, 98–99
conquest of New Carthage,
85–87
defeats Carthage, 89–92
meeting with Hannibal, 95–98
as military genius, 94
receives Roman triumph, 103,
104
rescues father, 64
"scorched earth" plan, 77
sea battles, 31, 32–34
Second Punic War, 39–40, 100–101
Seleucia, 106
Sempronius Longus, 65–66
Servilius, 69
ship construction, 31, 32
Sicily, Roman war in, 30, 32–35
Silenus, 22
sisters, 37
slavery, 29
slingers, 18–19
Socrates, 107
soldiers, 18–19, 30, 61
Sophonisba, 86–87
Spain. *See also* Iberian campaign
Hannibal as commander of, 39
Scipio as commander of,
84–85
Sparta, 31
speeches
before crossing Alps, 50–51
in New Carthage, 21–23

to Scipio, 97–98
at Tarentum, 81
strategies. *See* military tactics
Suppululiuma II, 31
Surus (elephant), 19, 24
Syphax, 86–87

T

tactics. *See* military tactics
Tanit, 46
Tarentum, 78–82, 84
temples, 47
Third Punic War, 108
Ticinus River, battle at, 62–64
tophet, 47
Trebbia, battle at, 66–69
triumph ceremony, 103, 104
truces with Rome, 92, 103–104
Tyre, 26, 27, 106

U

Utica, 90

V

Varro, C. Terentius, 70–71, 72
Volcae tribe, 45–48

W

war. *See also* Punic Wars
ancient role of, 14
inevitability of, 30
war ships, 31, 32
Washington, Denzel, 16–17
weapons
of mercenary army, 18–19
of Roman soldiers, 61
wife, 18, 38

X

Xanthippus, 34

Z

Zama, battle of, 98–101
Zuma aftermath, 102–104

ABOUT THE AUTHORS

◆ ◆ ◆

CLIFFORD W. MILLS is a writer, teacher, and editor who lives in Jacksonville, Florida. He has written biographies of Angela Merkel, Derek Jeter, Bernie Williams, Pope Benedict XVI, and Virginia Woolf. He has also compiled a volume of essays about J.D. Salinger, and has been an editor for John Wiley and Sons and Oxford University Press. Mills currently teaches at Columbia College in Jacksonville.

ARTHUR M. SCHLESINGER, JR. is remembered as the leading American historian of our time. He won the Pulitzer Prize for his books *The Age of Jackson* (1945) and *A Thousand Days* (1965), which also won the National Book Award. Professor Schlesinger served as the Albert Schweitzer Professor of the Humanities at the City University of New York and was involved in several other Chelsea House projects, including the series *Revolutionary War Leaders*, *Colonial Leaders*, and *Your Government*.